More Than Land

More Than Land

STORIES OF NEW ENGLAND
COUNTRY LIFE AND SURVEYING

Heman Chase

FOREWORD BY LAEL WERTENBAKER
WOOD ENGRAVINGS BY RANDY MILLER

William L. Bauhan, Publisher
DUBLIN, NEW HAMPSHIRE

Library of Congress Cataloguing in Publication Data
Chase, Heman: More than land
1. Chase, Heman.   2. Surveying.   3. New England History.
I. Title
TA533.C47A33   974.3′04′0924 (B)   74-78070
ISBN 0-87233-031-1

This book was set in Baskerville type
at Bayfield, Providence, R.I. and printed at
the Colonial Press, Clinton, Mass. U.S.A.

To the Memory of
WALTER AND MARGARET HARD
Late of Manchester, Vermont
Whose love, faith, good counsel and good cheer
will always be remembered with gratitude
and
whose warm-hearted and discerning stories of
the earlier people of their region
independent in thought and action
long encouraged me to record my own
experiences and contacts

Books by Heman Chase

American Ideals

Railroad Passenger Travel

Short History of Mill Hollow

More than Land

Contents

Foreword

IF YOU THINK the breed of writers who could tell you stories with pith and point for your pleasure has vanished from the earth, here is proof to the contrary. No wonder artist Randy Miller could not resist illustrating this series of adventures, vignettes, sketches of people, anecdotes and vivid, descriptive passages about the land, known as only, perhaps, a surveyor-by-profession can know land.

You may already be a friend of the author's. Heman Chase has more friends than any man I know. If you aren't, after you read this book you will be. It is as near, he says, to an autobiography as he intends to write—but the man he is is here in the telling, and that man is a friendly, observant, humorous, life-loving man.

He is a surveyor, trusted by the land, the law and his clients. His New England terrain is rugged, cranky and varied and he still clambers its heights and plunges through its thickets as if he were twenty-four instead of seventy-four. His profession provides the continuity for his literary journey in this book, but he often strays to explore by-paths among his interests. These interests are so diverse and his skills so abundant that he deserves to be called a renaissance surveyor—of life as well as land.

There must be something about New England that is delimiting. More often than elsewhere, you do find people with such rare combinations of talents and qualities. People with deep roots and ranging minds. Sturdy natural survivors with delicate and various tastes. . . . Has it to do with the intense variety of the weather?

In East Alstead, New Hampshire, near where he was raised, Heman Chase lives today. There's very little in the county, the state and the region he isn't part of. He is son of a doctor who had been educated at Harvard and in Europe. He was moved to New Hampshire very young. His mother, a school teacher, remarried in 1910, this time an architect from Harvard. When Russell Scott, the former headmaster of Bedales School in England, came to live nearby, Heman's mother, stepfather and father combined to persuade the distinguished educator to tutor Heman and his sister for nine enlightening months. (See "Earliest Lesson.") Then Heman went away to the George School, a Quaker institution in Pennsylvania, and after that to the University of Wisconsin.

As a graduate in civil engineering, "the Chase boy" came back to practice his profession at Bellows Falls and East Barnett, Vermont until the depression wiped out employment for young civil engineers. He married Edith Newlin, the permanent lady of his heart. She was a school teacher like his mother and so he taught school also. "Best thing that ever happened to me," he says, "next to marrying my wife. Teaching small children changed my view of life and I got interested in *everything* and in people of *all* ages."

In 1937 the Chases moved for good to Alstead and built their own house from which Heman went forth to survey land for a living. Independence—right down to cutting his own firewood for his own wood furnace—became the most important thing in the world to him. Except for two years as a draftsman and machine designer he never worked again on a corporate payroll.

Heman Chase always took inspiration where he happened to find it. His lifelong passion for music began with an Edison record of Verdi's *Cara Nome*, which he played over and over until he began to like it. Reading Henry George at the age of fifteen started him off philosophizing, and the philosophy of Henry George has colored everything he has thought since. As a young man he saw a tablet on the Williams Monument in Rockingham, Vermont, and decided poetry was a world to explore. In 1954 the Bellows Falls *Times* published his poem about that tablet and this led to more poems over the years. After he read the stories by Walter Hard of Manchester, Vermont, about country people, Heman wrote up a "hellishly funny yarn" about his own neighbors (see "Land Enough") and showed it to the Hards. They told him to go on writing. And he has.

This is his fourth book and he plans another one. He wishes he had more time for poetry, but he is still mighty busy working. He also teaches groups of children who gather around him as if he dispensed maple sugar instead of skills, writes and sees his many friends, attends every concert in this region rich in music, takes care of his house and land. There's no time in his life to be bored or gloomy.

If his view of life is a rosy one and his choice of what he writes about unfashionably warm and kindly, it's not because he doesn't observe and think about "a sick and bewildered world and society." He merely lacks one talent—for despair.

"Life owes me nothing," Heman Chase wrote to me in one of his welcome letters. "I have been most blessed. And no man could possibly have found a more congenial calling than land surveying in New Hampshire and Vermont. It has been for me over the past forty-six years a chance to survey more than land— people, problems, history, the terrain of God's country and Man's enhancement or desecration of it, and his joys, sorrows, successes, failures through life in the constant battle with Nature and his own shortsightedness or wisdom."

Herein are stories he has chosen from his life to share with us who are, or who will become, his friends. If the book makes you feel like writing to him, as it probably will, do. You may get in return one of his enchanting letters about, well, the weather, children, philosophy, economics, woodworking, music or whatever. Perhaps it will be in rhyme. The letter will cheer your day.

LAEL WERTENBAKER

Author's Note

WITH ONLY one or two exceptions, these stories and sketches originated directly in my own professional life as a land surveyor or in my long residence in a very small rural community.

If the collection as a whole seems to lack literary unity or internal consistency, that will simply be a revealing reflection of the wide variety of unexpectedness with which the incidents of my life and work have constantly confronted me, paralleling the people, the varied activities, and even the fickle weather of northern New England, the region that has most dominated my life.

I have been fortunate, through my working life of fifty years or so, to have experienced all sorts of situations in work, in environment, in natural setting, and in human contacts. I have dealt closely with clients as individuals who thus became friends in most cases, this last factor creating a sense of community between us, a sense which, when contemplated in the context of the larger business world, has revealed to me how much most people are missing.

In the course of each year's work, I have been able to survey much more than land. History, local customs, antiquities, human relations, geology and ecology could all be taken in as rich incidental rewards.

Such favor of destiny has "followed me" just about "all the days of my life", and should be regarded as very rare and precious in this modern age of specialization, urbanization, and mass means of intellectual homogenization. So if many of my stories seem to contain considerable background or descriptive matter, it is given for the deliberate purpose of sharing with readers some of the richness of detail of the ways and the atmosphere of an earlier age now passing with my generation—an age which, however, is of increasing interest to many who are fast becoming disenchanted with much of modern times and headlong "progress".

Sitting with Walter and Margaret Hard in their cozy little book-lined den in the rear of their wonderful old house in Manchester, Vermont, during the last twenty-five years of their lives —times that are still vivid and treasured memories for me—I shared with them many discussions about life and about authentic treatment of subject matter. And we agreed that, as the lives of most people were increasingly becoming just a vocational routine and society more commercialized and structured, it was getting harder to pick up actual stories or to have actual experiences of the old kind—from the days when life was more often a single-handed battle with Nature, conducive to that "independence of thought and action" that gives lasting value and character to the written recollection of human incidents.

The Hards' way of writing of events and people always appealed to me. It revealed the life, the work and the thought of earlier times and rural places then passing with them—or long since passed—and it was always appreciative, sympathetic, discerning, appropriate and true. So it was natural that I should feel their influence as friends, as philosophers and as writers.

These stories, except for a few judicious substitutions of names, places or insignificant details, are true to the facts just as closely as I could ascertain them at the time or recall them later while writing. By firm intention, they are free from any added literary or dramatic embellishment, the actual events and subject matter in every case being given as authentically as possible, seeming alone sufficient for their lasting interest and value.

HEMAN CHASE

Mill Hollow
February, 1975

More Than Land

Earliest Lesson

PROBABLY not many people, who have based a long professional career on some specialized interest, can pinpoint just when or how that interest was first implanted in their minds. But I think I am among those who can.

About the time I was through grade school, Russell Scott, former headmaster of Bedales School for Boys in England, came to America and bought a place near ours at Alstead, New Hampshire. My parents found him to be a true intellectual, a gifted teacher of many subjects, and a widely traveled citizen of the world, and arranged for him to act as private tutor for my sister and me. He taught us in separate sessions of two hours or so daily, during many memorable months, beginning in the fall of 1914.

With me, Russell took up English, French, mathematics, general science, and numerous miscellaneous concepts, all calculated to stimulate interest and curiosity. And in so doing, he gave me samples of his educated and humane view of the world.

Sometimes at the end of a session he would stump me with a riddle, asking me to have an answer for him the next day. One example I recall was this: He said, "Literary scholars now think that it is possible that the works of the famous Greek poet, Homer, were not written by Homer after all but by another man of the same name. Tomorrow, see if you can tell me what is funny about that."

He told me of discussions in English scientific circles of possible ways of communicating the facts of our existence and intelligence on this earth to the people, if any, on Mars for example. How could we communicate, and how might these presumed Martians respond in some way that we could understand and inform us of their culture. We would have to display in a visible manner, but of course not in words, some fact of universal validity. The theorem of Pythagoras had been decided upon; and a right-angle triangle with squares on each side would be constructed on a vast scale and executed in striking colors of planted foliage. Then our scientists would watch through the most powerful telescopes for some response of the Martians. Russell asked me to consider whether this could be done.

Russell was devoted to world peace, and to that end he was an active member in the society for the promotion of Esperanto, the universal language, and gave me numerous lessons with practice sessions.

Late in the winter of 1915, Russell came into the room one morning, evidently in a disturbed state of mind. He showed me a book, just received in the mail from England, entitled *German Atrocities*, recounting the horrible things alleged to have been done by the German army while smashing through Belgium.

"This is what is known as propaganda," he said. "The German people did not want war any more than the English. But when my government went to war with them, just like any government wishing its people to work, sacrifice, and fight some foreign country, they had to stir up their people's hate and fear by just such concoctions as this."

Thoughtfully perusing the pages of the book, reading excerpts here and there, he finally said, "My goodness! Wouldn't you think the English people would wonder how the Germans would have had time to do all this already." (Later that year he made a short trip back to England and, checking what stories he could, found them to be groundless.)

Looking back on this tutoring experience with Russell Scott, reminds me of President James A. Garfield's comment about one of his teachers at Williams: "A log with a student on one end and Mark Hopkins on the other is my ideal college."

But the most enduring experience I had with Russell was the day he announced that we would go out and measure a distance by triangulation.

Standing in a field (I can see it as I write this) he pointed across our pond to Mr. Spurr's cottage and said, "We cannot, of course, walk from here to there, but we can measure how far it is." At Russell's house we got his wheelbarrow, a wooden box, a sheet of brown paper and tacks to attach it to the top of the box, and a tape, ruler, pins, pencil, and two stakes. We laid off a measured base line in the field with a stake at each end. Laying off the base line to scale on the paper with pins at each end, we then set the whole crude equipment over each stake in turn, oriented the paper base line with the staked base line at each point, taking ruled sights to a corner of the cottage. This operation, obviously, gave us the basic data for the determination, by graphic means, of the distance from our location to the cottage: the measured base of a triangle and two adjacent angles. Then we repaired to the Scott kitchen. I don't know what Margaret Scott thought of the marks on her floor, but Russell (taking the part of the Biblical Mary rather than Martha) tacked the brown paper to it, and with a pencil and straight-edge we extended the cottage sight lines on the floor till they met. That point of intersection, I realized, represented the corner of the cottage, and the lengths of lines to it the distances, which we then scaled.

This brilliant scientific measurement thrilled me as nothing had before: a distance of 1500 feet or more, through intraversable space, and across water! For me, at the age of thirteen, this revelation was the starting point of a long series of similar projects initiated by myself—resulting after a few years in an engineering degree at the University of Wisconsin, and in the end a lifetime career as a surveyor.

I ran all the way home, burst into the house and cried, "Mother, I have just learned how to do the most wonderful thing!"

"What is that?" she asked.

"How to measure a distance without going there!"

Devil's Lake

DURING my first summer at the University surveying camp at Devil's Lake, Wisconsin, one project assigned to each pair of students was to survey a long, mountainous ground profile. From the top of a rocky cliff, it extended down the face and a treacherous talus slope, across an old lane to the top of a bank, down the bank to lake level, and then under the water and out along the bottom. Each man then made his own drawing of the results, lettering it all up in appropriate manner, the whole executed in India ink on regular "profile" paper.

While doing this office part of the work one evening in our tent, I yielded to a sudden impulse to embellish the drawing with a carefully made broadside view of a fish at mid-depth of the lake in several colors of ink. I thought the whole effect very natural, interesting and pleasing.

In the morning when I submitted the work to Mr. Wesley, he found my drawing conformed to past students' surveys of the same profile line, and he observed that it was a good job worth a grade of ninety-eight. But in his customarily humorless manner, he said that fish would have to come out! Weakly, I tried to defend it and protested the hazards of erasing from such thin paper. George Reed, an assistant instructor, who disliked Wesley, had been listening in on all this.

He strode over, glared at Wesley, and said to me, "Heman, don't you give in!"

But disregarding Reed, Wesley said sternly, "You heard me," and left the camp for the day with a group of students.

I was so angry at this point that I decided to appeal to Professor Ray S. Owen.

"Professor Ray"—as we always called him—was head of the

camp; back at Madison he was a director of the College of Engineering, and was Assistant Dean of Men for the University. He had the reputation for being a stern and thorough teacher, a hard task-master, but fair, and with a keen sense of humor. He was the sort of teacher who, though he drives you hard in school, will gain your liking in time, and does indeed gain your respect and appreciation forever for lessons that prove valuable and important later in practical life. In his Madison office, admonishing a student, he would often point to one of the numerous wise sayings posted on the wall, that might be appropriate to the fellow's case and tell him to read and ponder it. (I still recall two of them. They were by Elbert Hubbard. One was: "Those who never do any more than they are paid for never get paid for doing any more than they do." The other: "An excuse is the reason given for something which, if it had not happened for that reason, would have happened for some other.")

At his camp office, when he saw my drawing, Professor Ray agreed it was a good neat job, and was even mildly amused by the fish. But when I asked what to do about Mr. Wesley's ultimatum, he replied, "I can't settle any such question as that. It's between you and him."

Then, pausing, he added in a reflective tone, "I didn't ask to have Wesley here. The University sent him, assigned to teach topography. So, you and I have to get along with him. But I'll tell you something: he isn't any worse than lots of men you'll have to get along with when you get out in the world. So, if you learn to satisfy him, the lesson will be very valuable to you all your life. And another thing: lots of times, as in stupid little arguments like this, you can very well say, 'All right, Mister, you can have it your way.' You will not have lost face, you need not be ashamed, because you will have been the one big enough to rise above the pettiness of the situation; you will have ended the argument so you could get on with the next thing. That's what it is to be practical."

Fifty years have proven him right!

As the visit ended, he said, "Now as I told you before, I can't settle matters between you and Wesley. I hope you can. Good luck."

The fish came out at once; when submitted, the drawing was accepted—and graded, ninety-eight.

The Rat Race

WHEN I was nine we moved into a large old "four-square" brick house in a tiny hamlet long known as Mill Hollow, which at one time had been the early industrial center of East Alstead, New Hampshire. The house had been built in 1820 by Squire Ezra Kidder, a noted citizen of the "East Part" of the town and owner and operator of several of the small mills on the brook across the road and downstream from the outlet of Warren's Pond.

The bricks for our old house, had been made a mile and a half away in Breed's ancient, boggy meadow with its rich bed of clay (one of the virgin grass intervales found in 1753 by our town's first explorers). The house still had its original small-paned windows set in the deep recesses of the thick walls. It had very artistic interior mouldings and trim, "Christian" doors, and other modestly aristocratic features. Built after the age of huge central chimneys, the main part of the house was heated—to the extent that it was—by relatively small fireplaces built with their chimneys integral with the brick ends of the house. Of these there was one in the parlor, one in the living room, and upstairs one in each bedroom, north and south.

We children loved to explore the cellar, attics, wooden ell, attached barn and henhouse, all with their numerous closets and built-in cupboards and semi-secret cubbyholes. Among our discoveries was a box of old letters on a high shelf in a dark hall closet, revealing something of the life of the first owners. And the ancient newspapers covering the shelves made fascinating reading too. At first the whole place reeked of that musty smell of old houses long closed up, giving me a life-long impression of rural history. We often pondered how much this one, in its four and a half score years, had known of human life with its joys and sorrows, work and play, comings and goings, births and deaths. The old letters—many practically illegible—gave us some idea of what went on among the original owners, a devoted family of parents and their twelve children, around 1845.

My stepfather, a retired architect and antiquarian, easily discerned the methods of the house's construction, with its hand-hewn beams, mortise-and-tenon connections; the lathwork of split, thin hemlock; the numerous "cut" nails with a few handmade nails of an earlier age here and there. The boards showed the straight-across marks of the old up-and-down saw of the former mill built in 1770 just down the brook. He made all these features clear to us. In these ways did the old house yield up the many memories it held within its walls.

It was at least a century after 1820 that such things as insulation and "fire stops" became common in house construction. Spaces between wall and floor joists were anything but "dead air"; circulation was free and drafty. Cool, damp drafts came up into the dim attic of the ell from between the two-story vertical studs of the north wall. To my child's mind they brought with them the vague mysteriousness conveyed by Sir Walter Scott's "steep, winding, narrow stairways and dark communicating passages and cold and secret chambers deep down within the mysterious inner recesses of the castle." Indeed, these spaces, inadvertently left by early carpenters and supplemented by many narrow holes and gnawings, constituted a veritable paradise of freedom, travel, and dominion for generations of self-invited, intramural, four-legged, long-tailed residents who were here ahead of us.

Our mother was death on rats and mice, but beginning the year we came, it was a long, hard battle.

At a reasonable hour each evening, I would be given a "candle lantern" and sent up to bed in the chilly "southroom," later to be called when it was time to put out the light. And then it was that I, lying awake in the dark, would become keenly conscious of the strenuous nightly activity overhead! My idea of the actual number of rats and mice taking part was, no doubt, an exaggeration, but the mental picture of them was, and remains now, very vivid. I could just see that solid phalanx—two and a half feet wide, the width of the joists in the ceiling—as with loud squealing, scratching, twittering, and scampering they would race back and forth the whole length of my pitch dark room, regroup, fight, or just mill around, then charge off again. Was it a game, or savage conflict over prestige or bits of something stolen and eatable? Was there a competitive spirit, or just humor and exuberance? Exercise to keep warm? How I wondered and wondered what all the rushing about was for! At times they noisily scampered, as a mob with a destination, westerly to the holes and passages leading into the ell attic, and then a silence, as I pictured the entire tribe taking the long trip—by paths they knew by heart—way down and out to our grain bins in the stable. If I were awake when they returned, I listened to them surge again intermittently back and forth and round about, squeaking and scratching, singly or in great numbers, throughout the night.

Those many nights in childhood, sixty years ago, as I lay awake trying to visualize this mindless revelry, up overhead "where the action was," often come back to mind when viewing the human scene—folks milling about in Grand Central Station, on football fields, in subways, on throughways, or as protesting masses—or when contemplating the competitiveness of business and society or plans for the SST or reaching the Moon. I am sure that very few have any better illustrated concept of the term "Rat Race" than I!

Valuable Counsel from Uncle Jim

THE WILLIAMS HOUSE, in Bellows Falls, Vermont was always a warm and cheerful center of sociability for the many friends, young and old, of Uncle Jim and Aunt Sarah, or Auntie Williams as she was called by some.

She was the daughter of a ship's captain, and their long living room was amply decorated with elaborate silverware, pictures, and furniture her father had collected in the Orient. Her great delight was luscious cooking; on the many occasions when, surveying in that vicinity, I would drop in and join them with my paper-bag lunch, she would always supplement whatever I had with some sumptuous dessert—or a whole meal if I had let her! This informal, homey association began when I was a young surveyor and went on for years.

Uncle Jim, a retired banker, combined eager sociability, humor, and wisdom in business and human affairs. His sense of perspective and relaxed consideration of whatever you may have discussed left you feeling less worried or annoyed, more at ease and amused, by perplexing problems or people. I always came away feeling good, set up anew. He and the entire circle of their friends suffered a tragic loss when a stroke practically terminated his powers of speech, largely shutting off forever the rich, philosophic interchange of previous years.

During the early prime of his retirement, on one of these informal visits, I mentioned that in a few days I would be going to court in Keene, New Hampshire to show a map and give testimony about the conditions at the scene of a highway accident. Right away Uncle Jim asked, "Have you ever been in court before?"

"No," I said. "This is the first time."

"Then I think there are a few things I ought to tell you." He indicated two chairs and started deliberately to fill and light his pipe.

"Do you know what an advocate is?" he asked.

I had to admit that I did not.

"An advocate is somebody who defends or pleads the cause of another. Now, in this case, each of the contending parties will have hired a lawyer to present his side of the argument to the court. Each of these lawyers is his client's advocate and will do all he can to help his client win; in court he is completely biased in everything he does and says, in favor of his client, of course. And that is all right; that is what the public and court expect him to do and is all according to the accepted rules of litigation and the game of courtroom law practice. Of course, it is understood that his one-sided presentation of the case will be balanced by the opposing lawyer and his clients taking an equally biased view of the case in their favor. Then the judge and jury can decide which of the contending parties has put on the best, or most convincing, show, and award a decision accordingly.

"But when *you* go into a court case, your position is entirely different; you are *not* an advocate. You are what is called an 'expert witness,' supposed to know just how to make measurements and draw maps. The public and the court have a right to expect that you will testify as to the facts just exactly as you found them, leaving it up to the court and jury to decide what your evidence may prove.

"The lawyer who hires you as an expert witness may perhaps try to get you to slant your testimony in favor of his clients, in little ways that may not be noticed or challenged, but that is a temptation you must never yield to. You may have a feeling that, since a lawyer or his client is paying you, you should try to help them in their contentions as to the case. But that is wrong. Have it understood at the beginning of any court case that you know your position and your duty.

"What you are to do is simply to give the facts as you find them, and let the chips fall where they may. That is your duty to

10

yourself and to the public. And doing it, you will never get into trouble in court."

No better words were ever spoken to a young surveyor.

In all ages men have in times of stress sought fervently to invoke wisdom or power from sources outside of themselves.

In order to buck up their spirits, in the Civil War men sang "Just before the battle, Mother, I am thinking most of you."

At the great ski-jumping contests at Brattleboro, I have seen Catholic men and boys cross themselves just as they started down the slope.

Others, on approaching human situations expected to be contentious and difficult, have said, "I hope I will be able to think of what Dale Carnegie would say!"

In my experience, in the thirty-five or forty occasions when I have been involved in lawsuits, at the pre-trial conferences or on actually entering the courthouse, I have been fortified by recalling from my subconscious mind—and uttering them to myself—the words I spoke that day many years ago: "Thank you, Uncle Jim; I will remember what you say."

News Where it is News

In November 1927, we had the first of a series of great floods on the Connecticut River, the highest since 1869. I was working at the time as an "instrument man" with the engineers of the New England Power Company on the construction of the new hydro-electric station at Bellows Falls, Vermont.

This place had had a long history, first of the works of Nature, later of those of Man.

A rock barrier in the valley had created a cascade down which the river made an original descent of about forty feet over a distance of a third of a mile, from a stretch of stillwater above, down through rapids and chasms, to the famous "pool" below. The vast congregations of shad in this pool and the eastern salmon easily speared in the narrow channels in the rocks above, together attracted annual fishing parties of Indians three centuries ago whose "picture writing" on the ledges is still faintly visible today.

These ledges securely supported the first bridge ever to span the Connecticut River at any point, in 1785. They also occasioned the building, with English capital, of one of the very earliest barge canals in America, opened in 1802, with nine locks and total lift of forty-five feet, to be owned and operated by what was long known as the "Company for Rendering Connecticut River Navigable by Bellows Falls." By 1860 river barging had been replaced by railroads which found this a natural and economic place for secure bridge foundations and as a junction of two important through lines: one between Boston and Rutland and the Champlain valley; the other from New York and New Haven, to Montreal. But by the time the canal was no longer used by barges it had gained a new importance in the development of water power for the mills, which brought fame and fortune to the town as a center for pulp and paper. At the height of this development of industry here, it was estimated that 13,500 horse-power was produced by seventy separate turbines in the various mills.

Our work here for the power company was intimately involved with all these works of Man and Nature.

The plans of the power company (which were brought to completion the following year, with the new station in production of electricity—"on the line" as power men say) included the following: (1) purchase of all power rights in the canal and mill properties; (2) building a new dam on top of the old, equipped with the latest flood-passing apparatus (roller gates); (3) the modernizing and enlarging of the canal to a width of a hundred feet and depth of twenty four; (4) and the building of a new power house equipped with three turbines of about 18,000 horse-power each, operating under a final head of about sixty-two feet. Most of my work was laying out "line and grade" for general alignment and concrete work in the canal and on the dam.

The heavy rains of many previous days of that fall of 1927 had raised all waters in the valley and its entire watershed to record heights. At this point the river, in height and volume of discharge, was to exceed the previous record of 1869.

By noon, on Friday, November 4th, the river, still rising, had already torn out a large area on the New Hampshire side, including the eastern approach to the steel-arch highway bridge at North Walpole, exposing its pile foundation and revealing the prehistorically smoothed ledges of an earlier glacial-age bed of the stream.

After this, I heard someone speak in a kindly manner to George Roland, one of our older men, saying, "I'm sorry you lost your house, George." "My house!", George said, "Hell, I lost my lot, too!" His was only one among three houses and one of our construction shanties that were also carried down river and broken up.

The water over-topped and broke through the coffer dam at the head of the canal, flooding our unfinished work there, and at the lower end—though our powerhouse construction stood

13

firm—the current turned to right and to left, venting its grim, blind force down through the exposed and vulnerable paper mills. At the site of the new dam, the flood waters tore out concrete form work or shifted it beyond repair, and our new foundation pits, laboriously excavated down to good clean ledge, were filled with gravel. Later we had to make a foundation of wood piles and steel sheet piling under part of the dam at that site, as the only means of restoring our work to its place in the general time schedule of the entire project.

Communication from outside the town was delayed or cut off by the halting of vehicles and trains. The storm brought down telephone and electric wires, poles and all; highways were buried, undermined or washed out; railroad embankments were washed away by the swift powerful current, in places leaving tracks suspended in mid-air or tipped up on edge.

Although the river, steadily rising at about a foot an hour, threatened to destroy all in its path, the town fought back—in a combined effort by local citizens and men from the mills, the power company, the utilities and the railroad. The railroad bridges, over the river and across the canal down in the center of the village, were weighted down with freight cars. The railroad tunnel beneath the Windham Hotel and the village square was barricaded with timber and sandbags. That afternoon the water pouring down the canal began washing away the west approach to the new concrete arch bridge at Bridge Street; so a steam shovel was set up at a gravel bank on Rockingham Street, and from then on, all Friday afternoon and night, fifteen dump trucks in steady succession roared down through the village square to pour their loads into the breach.

These desperate efforts were almost all successful, even though the water did not reach its peak at Bellows Falls till the end of the afternoon and for a few hours maintained a peak level of about twenty-six feet above the old dam (about thirteen feet higher than water is held north of the new dam today.)

Naturally this was not the only place to suffer from widespread floods. In one way, the misfortune of others worked to our benefit! An express train from Boston, with two carloads of fresh meats and other groceries bound for Rutland and Burlington,

14

could get no further than Bellows Falls. So those cars were opened up, and the perishable but welcome commodities were distributed to local stores. The schools were let out—surely there could have been little if any concentration then—so that for once the children could see history in the making. Altogether, this event must have been the most exciting for Bellows Falls since July 8, 1840, when Daniel Webster—returning from his famous rally at Stratton—spoke in the town square to a political gathering of three thousand.

During lunch hour on the 4th, our employer, the company's resident engineer Robert F. Olds, asked for two parties of volunteers—one to go up river and the other down—to observe the height and time of the passing of the "peak" of the flood at two different points he designated. Some offered to go down in the Brattleboro direction, and I—speaking for myself and for my then greatest pride and joy, my 1924 Buick Master Six Touring Car—offered to make the northern trip to Ascutneyville Bridge. My fellow volunteers were George C. (Ben) Benjamin and a rodman named Moody. I knew all the roads—or said I did—and assured him we would cover the twenty-two miles in time to accomplish the purpose. Mr. Olds, with his knowing half-smile, said that whatever the cost of mileage, time or damage proved to be, he would see that the company paid me well. And later, always a man of his word, he did.

After taking a few instruments from the office and making a tour of our respective rooming places for whatever overnight gear we might need, we set out.

I regret not taking any notes in those days, for the courses we attempted on that wild ride are now too vague for me to recall, except for some of the scattered incidents. But it was certainly a frantic search—you might say one of "probing" in one direction, then in another, or skirting around some real or rumored barrier—to find a route. But Ben claims to remember clearly—after four decades and more—all the main points on the route both up and back on the 4th and 5th of November. And my memory verifies his on most essentials.

To start north in the usual way on the Vermont side would have been out of the question; our knowledge of river levels

15

told us that the Williams River, a western tributary of the Connecticut, would surely be flooding the old Covered Bridge on the Missing Link Road (a stretch of U.S. Route 5).

So we crossed to the New Hampshire side through the old Tucker covered bridge and headed north toward Charlestown, but no sooner did we reach the first low section of road than we were faced with deep and impassable water. We turned around, passed by the Tucker Bridge and drove south on the New Hampshire side toward Cold River Station. Within a short distance we met deep water covering that road, and just as we were braking to a stop, my front right wheel dropped through the undermined edge of the road. Luckily, a big truck, just then turning back from the obvious but unpredictable hazards ahead, pulled us out. Back we drove to the Tucker Bridge and crossed into "the Falls" once more, to start all over again, on Vermont roads, whatever they might be like.

Even with Ben's letter of recollections, I have only a vague picture of how we went. Briefly, our route took us to Saxton's River and Chester. We wound through the Proctorsville Gulf, on our way to Cavendish; we were turned back at a washout, but it was just as well since the route east from that village had already gone down the Black River. Back in Chester, we drove to Springfield; then to Gould's Mills where we turned north and went up over hilly, rough, muddy, back roads—and one pasture lane by-pass—and did at last reach the little village of Ascutneyville as darkness closed down, after going ninety-five confusing miles to reach a point normally twenty-two miles straight north from where we started.

We went straight down to the Connecticut River bridge, and from the bridge floor we let down the leveling rod to a flash-lighted spot on the black speeding current. The water passed just beneath us with a deathlike silence, broken only at instants by the little irregular sucking sounds of whirlpools intermittently forming at the corners of the old stone piers. We noted the rod reading.

The sense of urgency now past, we walked just a few steps back up the hill toward the village and made arrangements for staying the night at the Wilgus farm house; here we found a good and welcome supper.

16

Back at the bridge after supper, we repeated the measurement from floor to water surface and found it had gone down a little. The "peak" had passed Ascutneyville! We realized then, that we had probably failed to reach this point in the river valley soon enough for our first measurement to record the maximum stage of the water. But God knows we tried!

For awhile neither Moody, Benjamin nor I felt any inclination to take our turns at going to bed. We stayed on the bridge far into the November night, a night long cherished for its starlit natural beauty, its nearly uninterrupted opportunity for thought and reflection on Nature Irresistible—and Man for the moment, held waiting in abeyance.

We watched as a tall slim tree came floating down and lodged against the west abutment and lower steelwork of the bridge, where partly submerged and held there in the powerful grip of the stream with its largest and lowest branch it beat a weird, monotonous rhythm against the lower cord of the bridge truss, all night long.

The only human beings we saw or spoke with throughout the night were four fur-coated Dartmouth students. They arrived on the east end of the bridge on foot, coming there just to look around. They said they had been coming north, up the Connecticut valley heading for Hanover. In order to get across the Sugar River, a New Hampshire tributary entering the Connecticut just south of this bridge, they had gotten their old Model T Ford up onto the Boston and Maine Railroad tracks, and, jogging over the ties and astride one rail, had crossed over the Sugar River on the railroad's very well-named "High Bridge," getting off the tracks at the first grade crossing to the north. There have been many stories about the audacity of Dartmouth men—or boys—and their alleged deeds have at times been substantiated. I long remained skeptical about this particular exploit, but a man born and raised in that vicinity told me the young men might have accomplished it by means of a couple of farm lanes crossing the railroad "at grade," both north and south of the "High Bridge."

For the latter part of the night, we took our turns going down to the bridge to measure the receding level of the river.

After breakfast with the Wilguses, we started the long trip

back. Crossing this same bridge, then passing through Claremont, we journeyed south as best we could, mostly by back roads and through small places.

By mid-afternoon we had reached the valley of Cold River at some now-unrecalled point. This is another New Hampshire tributary of the Connecticut, entering at the south end of Fall Mountain and just south of Cold River Station. The road from Cold River, north to the Tucker bridge, was closed because of flood damage. So, leaving my car near the Station, we walked the last mile of our journey, following the Boston tracks of the railroad, north to the Tucker bridge, and crossed over into Bellows Falls.

We reported to Mr. Olds with the technical gauging data and a brief account of our adventures, and then went out to look over the wreckage wrought upon our works in the past thirty-six hours by the receding river, now deceptively innocent-looking.

I may continue to gradually forget details of those two memorable days of my connections with the New England Power Company during the Connecticut River flood of November 4th, 1927.

Of all things heard or seen, done or said in my experience at that momentous time, one will always remain clear. On the afternoon of the 5th while returning from Ascutneyville bridge to Bellows Falls, we stopped in the little village of Unity and went into the small general store. This was presided over by a little old lady—very old but sharp. We passed the time of day, asked about the road conditions ahead, and indulged our various desires for cigarettes, chocolate bars, and "belly wash".

Unthinkingly, I put my remarks about the recent weather in the form of a question, saying to the storekeeper, "Didn't you have an awful lot of rain up here in the last two weeks?"

With utter disdain, she said, "Well, I guess you ain't been readin' the papers lately!"

Several Lessons in One

MY FIRST SURVEY of any significance in a fair sized town was for the United States Post Office lot at Bellows Falls, Vermont at the time of its purchase by the Treasury Department in 1928.

To begin with, my preliminary survey of the buildings on the lot and the existing boundary and street lines all failed, in slight and varying degrees, to conform exactly with the ancient deed descriptions and measurements. Some of these went back well over a century, none of them the subject of the slightest controversy. Peaceful occupancy with things as they were had prevailed for as long as anyone in town could remember.

But the theoretical discrepancies caused a great show of official, time-consuming concern in Washington whence came our sheets of instructions for lot surveys, title searching and reconciliation.

Old "Judge" O'Brien—cantankerous, cynical, erratic, and gruff, then in part-time legal private practice—represented the owner of the lot who was under agreement to sell as soon as surveying and other legal and technical matters were accomplished. The work of satisfying the Treasury Department officers with all our work dragged on for months.

Mr. O'Brien's correspondence entailed a succession of ten letters, so he said, to Washington officials, every letter answered by a different man, and most of the replies bogged down in trivialities. None of this correspondence, of course, gave any sense of real "communication", or of "a meeting of minds", as we think of the full meaning and value of such things today. No one "down there" seemed to be "in charge" or to have any common sense. It all constituted my first real glimpse of what a vast, bureaucratic and bottomless rat-hole the Federal departments must be—and remember, this was forty-six years ago!

19

One technical requirement was to show "true bearings" of all boundary lines on the map and in the final description. These were to be determined by a telescopic sight on the North Star in conjunction with the various computations for knowing where the star was with respect to the Celestial North Pole at the exact moment of sighting. So I had to spend an evening, at the site, with the surveyor's transit set up on the edge of the sidewalk, peering at the Star and—since it was 43° up—getting a crick in my neck as I bent to put my eye to the telescope eye-piece.

With one hand I pointed a flashlight into the outer end of the telescope to light the cross hairs, and with the other turned the clamp and tangent screws of the instrument to make exact sightings. Now and then I would straighten up to read angles and record the exact time by my watch or to explain to late passers-by what in the devil I was doing there anyhow at such a time of night.

Nobody knows to this day whether I did this abstruse part of the work correctly, but over the many years since, the building has worked; they seem to distribute the mail there quite successfully, whether or not they know accurately which way is True North.

Washington required that all property corner monuments be of concrete, each one being so cast as to have one corner making the same angle as formed by the lines meeting at the property corner, and each one set within the property and so placed as to be flush with those lines and flush with the ground surface. (Standard practice calls for monuments to be set on private property, flush with the edges of public property—as indicated by sidewalks, etcetera—and centered on private property division lines.) Looking at a copy of the map, as I write this, I see that for once Washington did see fit to bow to God; at the northwest corner of the lot He had placed an immovable ledge, and I was allowed to place a concrete monument in a recorded position with respect to the exact corner and to mark that corner with an iron pin in a hole drilled in the ledge.

At last—July 30, 1928, so the map is dated—the survey was completed, the lot corners marked, the map drawn and ready for blueprinting and all other requirements met, except for the official signing of the map by the Town Manager.

Mr. O'Brien reached for the phone, gave the operator the town office number, and in a moment said loudly, "Ruggles? Tom O'Brien. I have the map of the new post office lot. It's all done except that you've got to sign it. . . . What? Listen, there's no ifs about it. . . . You will so sign it, and the surveyor's coming over right now. Goodbye."

Knowing how public officials can, if they wish to for personal reasons, "drag their feet" with respect to some duty, and never having previously met the town's new manager, I began to visualize the possibilities of still further delays due to unnecessary troubles with officialdom. The job was already running into the fourth month and with no money in sight until our client, the seller, got his money. Now, I thought, might not Mr. O'Brien's harsh and entirely uncalled-for manner of speaking to a high public officer simply cause further exasperating delay? This morbid thought plagued me all the way to the town hall.

But Mr. Ruggles received me most courteously. The rapport that one technically trained man feels for another seemed to grace the atmosphere at once and to bring us together. All my previous fears proved groundless. (In fact, though nothing was said about it that day, this meeting was ultimately to lead to much future congenial, profitable, instructive experience and employment by the very man I had at first approached with much apprehension.)

Looking over the map in question with due deliberation, Mr. Ruggles expressed entire approval of its general and technical completeness and hence its presumed accuracy. And with my steel pen and India drawing ink, he "signed on the dotted line" in the lower left-hand corner of the map in its original tracing cloth form.

Able at last to relax, I then said, "I greatly appreciate your willingness to sign the map. After hearing Mr. O'Brien speak to you on the phone as he did just now, I wondered whether we'd ever get your signature."

"Oh, that?", he said. "Shucks! I never let a little thing like that bother me!"

A Rural Genius

ERASTUS P. KIDDER (1840-1922), who had sold us our house in 1910, was one of our most illustrious neighbors. He lived next door and schooled us in the history of Mill Hollow. His old mill reflected many talents of mechanical self-reliance; and the restoration of its water power after some years of disuse was accomplished by himself and Carroll E. Hatch, his son-in-law who was to take over the mill and business. I was allowed to be around the job and to help in various small ways. And in 1914, the building of a dam, a flume, a penstock, and water wheel, all based on Mr. Kidder's ideas, was the beginning of my engineering education and life-long study of water power. The entire conduct of the work was proof of the all-round practical abilities of "the old man," as Carroll called him.

The progressive powers of self-made men, however, are sometimes limited by various personal factors, or ignorance of scientific theory, or just plain stubbornness, as illustrated by two of my memories of "Rat," or "Rastus," as he was generally called. One of these was his quite rationally thoughtout Perpetual Motion Machine. Years ago, it seems, generous rewards were offered to encourage inventors in this "scientific" endeavor; I do not know whether that was any part of the motivation in his case.

My father took me with him to call on Mr. Kidder, in the summer of 1909, I think, especially to see this machine, then being much discussed in the community. I well remember the neatly made and delicately balanced wheel, with its dozen or so firm, flat, wooden spokes, and, between each of them and swinging from one to the other, an equal number of intermediate, movable, lead-weighted spokes made from some of Mrs. Kidder's old corset stays. How smoothly it would turn with a fascinatingly rhythmic clickety-click when given a little push. Of course, disappointingly, it always gradually slowed down and finally came to a gentle stop. Mr. Kidder explained the physical principle he was invoking (which we realize now was false), namely, that a weight, repeatedly falling, always imparts, to whatever it strikes, an amount of energy greater than that required to gently lift it back up each time to its initial position. He assured us that this wheel would run forever as soon as he was able to make some absolutely frictionless bearings. Logic pointed that way, certainly! My father, being a very considerate gentleman, expressed

sincere interest and respect; but after we left, he explained to me —though, of course, I could not then have fully understood it —the utter, theoretical hopelessness of all such "machines," even if based, as we know they were, on ideas that have intrigued the mind of Man from time immemorial and in centers of "philosophical" activity even greater than Mill Hollow!

Mr. Kidder was a stubborn, narrow-minded man, and he was very proud of the water wheel he had designed and helped build at the time of the restoration. When his son-in-law, Carroll Hatch, vowed he was going to make a change in the wheel, after about four years of growing dissatisfaction, the old man became scornful and difficult. At last Carroll decided that he knew enough and had the courage to buck the ridicule and dire predictions of "The old man," and he went off and bought a secondhand Tyler Turbine Water Wheel, made in Claremont, New Hampshire. When finally installed in the wheel pit and connected to penstock, main vertical shaft, and gate shaft, the new Tyler wheel had all the power, speed, and reliability that Carroll had hoped for. It amply justified the enthusiastic praise of fifty-three testimonial letters from satisfied users in an old copy of the Tyler catalog of 1869 and the favorable opinion of the Directors of the Holyoke Testing Flume as well.

But "The old man" remained critical—that is, he did up to the time of his ill-fated attempt to prove the new wheel a failure, inferior to the one he had designed.

As he shuffled into the mill one morning, he thought that Carroll, running the shingle saw in the far corner of the back room, had not seen him. After gazing down at one of the large main shaft pulleys not then in use but whirling in a hole in the floor, he brought in a piece of timber, thrust it into the hole and pried it down on the rim of the pulley, hoping to stop the mill machinery. Though bearing down on this lever with all his might, and as clouds of blue smoke from the scorching timber filled the air, he simply could not slow the machinery appreciably. Finally, giving up, throwing down the timber in disgust, and shuffling out, he was heard to mutter: "By Gad, there's power!" He never brought up the subject again.

Surveying and Farming

IRA SETH LITTLEFIELD was born and lived all his life in New London, New Hampshire. He died in 1957 at the age of eighty-four. He had attended Colby Academy in his home town, then a school for boys and girls, which later became Colby Junior College for Women. Some time after graduation, he took up land surveying as a sideline to his work and life on the farm. This was in an age when farming was still recognized as the foundation of rural life and such specialties as Ira's thought of as auxiliary activities.

For fifty dollars someone offered to sell Ira an old surveyor's transit, which, after getting the favorable opinion of his teacher of technical subjects at the Academy, he bought and used all his life. In later years this old instrument afforded some of his friends no little amusement. Having opposing tangent screws for both "upper" and "lower" motions, it required the use of both hands at once in making each sight. Also, it had no vertical circle or arc on the telescope axis, rendering it useless in operations involving inclined sights. I once asked Ira how he accomplished the variety of surveys indicated by his very fine letterhead. "Well, I'll tell you," he said, "when any of these city folks want a map of their place to show to some architect down country, I sketch in all the important things; I give them a few hand level sights here and there; then I talk 'em out of wanting anything else."

Ira's old transit had still other features of a museum-piece, but after a fashion, it served him—and to his entire satisfaction—during a professional career of sixty years.

Ira once paid a bitter price for using the old solid-leaf type of fieldbook. While surveying one winter on Otter Pond in Sunapee, New Hampshire, he broke through the ice. A rescue team got him out of the water and into the nearest house as fast as they could and dried him out by the stove. When he finally thought of it, he asked, "Where's my book?" Nobody had seen it during the excitement of the rescue, or since. It could not be found. Then Ira said, "Well, there goes the notes for my last 10 years of work in the town of Sunapee."

For the actual work and techniques of surveying, Ira's preparation and qualifications would rightly be adjudged "practical" in nature. Once during a lawsuit, while in court on the witness stand, he was asked where he had studied surveying. Triumphantly he bellowed his answer: "In the woods!" and brought down the house. Indispensable, of course, as such a training ground is, there might be some things not too readily learned there. One time he was trying to determine the south line of a property he had surveyed fifty years before. He ran from the road easterly quite a distance down through the woods toward the pond shore on the same compass bearing used previously, and ran smack into the boathouse of his client. The owner was much disconcerted, but being merely a graduate of the Julliard School of Music, was conscious of his ignorance of such matters. He did recall, however, hearing that needles were known to change, and with appropriate humility he asked Ira whether he had considered the effect of any possible change of the compass needle over the years.

"No I didn't," Ira said with finality, "it wouldn't have been enough to make a mite o' difference."

The owner wasn't in a position to argue against Superior Authority, and he submitted to Judgment. But years later a simple check showed that the change, generally known for the region, would definitely have made a difference sufficient to exonerate the boathouse.

Whatever technical shortcomings Ira may have had, were certainly counterbalanced by other factors. Among these were his thorough blazing of trees along lines in the woods, his setting of a large number of stone posts at property corners, and his great memory of locations once visited. He had the instinctive sense by which those of long experience can ferret out old, obscure or perhaps lost, evidences of boundaries long neglected. He became, during his lifetime, one of those one-man institutions so characteristic of the on-going stability and life of rural regions a generation ago and now rapidly passing. Most of his work extended over an area as wide as could be reached in a day by horses and carriages—without interfering too much with the constant chores and other duties at home. He said he guessed his "instrument" had "straddled" seventy-five percent of all the old "stakes and stones" at land corners in his own and the adjoining towns.

As he became less active in late life, younger surveyors working in the region often had to refer to Ira, for his memory, old notes, records, and maps. He did not have a car then (if ever he had one); but as he said, "If anybody wants me, they'll have to come and get me. They know where I am."

And certainly a visit at his place would long be remembered.

New London lies on a high open plateau, and Ira's house was about half a mile north of the village, off the main road and down a small dirt lane. Past some old maples, you drove around the south end of the house and then left through the rear yard, and there was the main—or at any rate the most used—entrance, with its broad, flat stone doorstep. Often as not ducks or hissing geese approached from the cluttered sheds and barn while you knocked at the door. Visitors would be welcomed by Ira's loud, booming voice and by a whiff of the physical atmosphere within as he opened the door and then led the way through a sort of catchall or anteroom and into the kitchen. There he would offer a chair as soon as one could be dumped out and set by the glowing wood stove.

How well I recall my first time there! Ira said, "I'm certainly glad to see you. Now just make yourself comfortable. You'll excuse me while I get my sister up; she'll want to see you, too." And he went into a bedchamber just off the kitchen and closed the door.

In the center of the kitchen was a large table with a small cleared space for eating at one end, but otherwise covered with the remains of past meals and a mow of old papers. On the first floor every room in this old, low, one-storied, beam-ceilinged farmhouse was piled high with stacks of old newspapers, cartons, boxes, broken furniture and Heaven-only-knows-what-all, so that among the clutter one picked his way from room to room along narrow paths. Ira's map work was done in a distant

27

south room on a small cleared space at one end of a large drawing board laid over two tall "horses". The rest of the drawing table was heaped with a deep conglomeration of maps, notebooks and odds and ends, and it supported a large kerosene lamp, the only type of lighting in the house. Over everything lay much dust, and through all ran the pervasive reek of vinegar, old pickles—in short, the common atmosphere of old farmhouses where men have to do all the inside and outside work.

But above the tangible grime and disorder rose the spirit of the inhabitants! After a time, the door to the bedchamber opened; backing slowly into the room, and holding both her hands gently, Ira led his sister—very old, very frail, but smiling —to her accustomed chair between the stove and table. With breath recovering, all faculties alert, she acknowledged the introductions eagerly. They both vied good-naturedly with each other in the questions, explanations, and irrelevant pleasantries of our first getting acquainted—she so delicate and light, and he by 14 years the younger, of large frame, bushy brows, and courteous but stentorian joviality—it was, indeed, a visit enjoyed by all and long to be remembered.

And with an unexpected note for me!

This was Dr. Anna Littlefield. She was 87 at the time. I was not to learn till later some of her life story, though even then I sensed it must be an unusual one. She, too, had attended Colby Academy. She taught several years in rural schools, and then returned to join the faculty of the Academy as its teacher of art. She was an excellent painter of biological specimens of the flora of the region, and did many fine oil portraits as well, as evidenced by a number of examples I saw long afterward. The great fire of 1892 destroyed the building housing her department. This event she interpreted as a divine suggestion that now was the time to take up another of her strong desires, that of being a doctor. She enrolled in the Women's Medical College of Pennsylvania, received her medical degree in 1895 and began practicing at once. She was, or so she believed, the first woman physician in New Hampshire, and served fifty-five years. In 1945 her alma mater presented her with a silver brooch for fifty years of continuous practice, and the same year the state Medical Society gave her a gold medal for a half century of membership.

Now her life appeared to be limited to the companionship with her brother, her flowers, pictures, clippings, memories, glimpses out the windows at the quiet scene—and these visits! Once in the fall she looked out eagerly and said, "How I should love to bring in an armful of these beautiful leaves!" A great lover of Nature, in a town of more than average sophistication, she had been the first president of its garden club. As for her religious affiliations, I am in doubt; but, later on, I learned that when Ira was asked if his sister had been a member of the Baptist Church, he had said, "No, I guess you can't rightly say so, but I think she went there enough to have gained squatters' rights."

When the "business" part of a visit, concerned with some specific property survey, finally had to be brought up, Ira would happily take over. A few seconds of thought, with screwed-up eyebrows, would "bring it all back" again. Yes, he could remember that sketch he had once made, or that map, or that description; and he would lead the narrow way to the office. Here he would rummage through the mow of material on the table; or pull out drawers, paw through boxes, books, files and cases. He would usually find the missing paper or map or notes here. But if he failed, he would straighten up—his eyes gleaming and a grim smile of determination on his face—and would announce recourse to the last resort—"a raid on the archives": the search through an old hair trunk in the attic, so he said. Excusing himself he would mount the stairs. I know of no instance of ultimate failure.

I was once engaged by a Mr. and Mrs. Collins to survey a tract of land on the shore of Lake Sunapee near George's Mills. The description of the land was not sufficiently specific regarding one of the lines. Hearing that a map of the land beyond that line had been made by Ira Littlefield, we decided to see it. So we went up to New London.

As usual, a pleasant visit preceded business—in fact, unusually pleasant, as this time a very attractive and relatively young lady was along who was a delight to Dr. Anna and a thrill to Ira, always a great hand with the ladies!

Ira said that "Yes," he could remember that location very well; he had set stone bounds at bends in the line thirty years before. No doubt, they were now covered up by the "down timber" of the 1938 hurricane so we could never find them without his help. He would go down there with us and resurvey those lines together. "But first," he said, grasping the astonished Mrs. Collins firmly by the arm, "I want to show you the view from my back meadow." And he marched her, followed by Mr. Collins and me, out the lane to a beautiful open knoll commanding a fine prospect to the north overlooking Pleasant Pond.

Down at Sunapee, Ira directed and encouraged our removal of brush. The post at the highest point in the line could, indeed, never have been found without his memory and persistence. By late afternoon we still had some distance yet to go to reach the shore, and Ira said, "We've got to hurry; I've got to get back and do my chores."

"Oh, I didn't know you had chores to do," I said.

"Why sure, I'm milking five cows right now."

Ira must have been seventy-five at that time. I said to him, "Well, Ira, don't you think it is high time you decided whether you are going to be a surveyor or a farmer?"

With a loud chuckle he said, "Oh, I decided that question years ago. I wanted to survey just enough so I could afford to live on the farm!"

Rare Wisdom

WHILE SURVEYING a village property, we found too little evidence on the land in the presumed vicinity of the north boundary line and too little information in the land records to enable us to mark the line and corners with any certainty. This was plainly a case where a line would have to be established by agreement with whoever owned the land adjoining.

That owner proved to be Will Gilman, probably in his seventies but still very active around his place. Over the phone I explained my problem.

"That won't be any great problem," he said. "You just come down here any time. I'm easy to get along with. If you are, too, we'll settle that line in no time."

It all worked out just as he predicted.

I have often thought how good it would be, how much trouble it would spare us, if we, while dealing with other people on common problems, could make a point of being, as old Mr. Gilman expressed it—and as he was that day—"easy to get along with."

Practical Sense in the Green Mountain State

IN HIS HOME TOWN of Chester, Vermont and its surroundings, I have found William Orcutt a great help in deed study and in the understanding and tracing out of old property lines on wood lots and abandoned farms. His mind seems to arrive at the essential considerations quicker than mine, so on the several jobs he has helped me with, he has expedited the work very greatly. Whatever the problem, he got at the heart of it promptly and stated it well.

For a summer and weekend retreat and speculative venture, a Mr. Romain, from New Jersey, bought about one hundred acres bordering on a backwoods section of the Popple Dungeon Road.

His regular work, "down country," was with one of the utility companies near his home, and much of his attention was devoted to the proper placement of poles. He was with Bill and me when we were about to set an iron stake where his land cornered at the road, and he asked how we were going to know exactly where to put it. I said we would put it in line with the property division wall (which stood some distance back in the woods) and at the edge of the right-of-way of the road, and that since the width of the public right-of-way of country roads of this class was three rods, we would put the stake about a rod and a half from the center of the "traveled way."

"I don't want any trouble with the town about this in the future," Mr. Romain said. "Where I come from, we have to survey out the legal location of a road, to be sure we are right."

"Well, I'll tell you, Mr. Romain," said Bill, "in Vermont a road is where it is."

The Vermont Seal of Purity

LATE one rainy afternoon in May, I stopped at a Vermont farmhouse to visit an old friend. To get in the door, where he stood welcoming me, I had to step carefully over quite a number of gallon cans, evidently of maple syrup, that were leaning against each other at odd angles, on the big stone doorstep, obviously getting wet.

After the usual pleasantries, catching up on events of recent months and so on, I asked what the syrup was doing out there in the rain.

In his usual, chuckling drawl, he said, "Well, I'll tell ye, I got an order for sixty gallons of syrup from a man down country. I didn't have quite enough of my own this year, so I had to go down the road a piece to my neighbor's and get fifteen gallons from him to fill out the order. That's what you see out there in the rain now. I thought that was the easiest way to get *his* labels off."

Who is My Father?

FOR MANY YEARS, on all my surveying trips I have carried in the car a long black box full of instruments and supplies for map making. On top of a compartment in the lid of the box is a row of professional registration and membership cards certifying my numerous affiliations, as well as a picture of my two daughters playing recorders together on the lawn, and a portrait of Henry George.

Mr. George was the greatest exponent of what I believe to be an economic reform that would improve the structure of society and the status of mankind more than any other single measure. My family brought me up in his philosophy, and I respect him deeply beyond words, indeed, actually—although he has been at rest for seventy-five years—to the point of affection as for a present, living person and spirit.

But I am also among those who bitterly regret the skepticism and ridicule brought on his doctrine by those of his ardent, overzealous followers who have, in the past, and in a boring, narrow-minded manner and with tedious, repetitious insistence, declared his idea to be—if their claims were all added up—the cure for practically all human problems.

One day I was studying land records in the Registry of Deeds at Newport, New Hampshire. My black box stood open on the table. One of my lawyer friends, Kenneth D. Andler, came in, greeted me and others and then looked over the pictures. He correctly surmised that the first was of my two beautiful daughters, and then said, "And who is this old man over here; is he your father?"

The next three seconds or so was one of those times when half a century of one's life, thoughts, and deepest feelings flash

34

past the mind's eye. I suddenly felt an inward amusement, realizing then in a split second why neither "Yes" or "No" would be complete and accurate. Of course, in the end I went ahead and stated only the literal truth: "No, that is Henry George."

However, if I had given a figurative—or otherwise qualified—answer, in recognition of the spiritual, philosophical, or intellectual phases of fatherhood, Ken Andler's reaction might have been little different from what it was.

"Henry George, Henry George," he said, with an air of wonder. "Well, well, well." Then drawing a deep breath, in measured tones and so that all in the room might have heard, he continued: "Heman Chase, at the drop of a hat, will tell you the cause and cure of all the world's troubles. . . . Oh, dear, dear, dear," then adding, "Just let me get to work," as he headed for the index volumes.

The Stranger

THE CUPOLA HOUSE in Mill Hollow, Alstead, originally built
as a fourteen-bedroom boarding-house in 1865, was the home of
Frank and Nettie Messer when we first came to this tiny hamlet.
Frank, who had been an active farmer and mill man, had died
in 1907. Nettie thereafter lived alone, taking few, if any, boarders.
Then in 1910 John Goode assumed the duties of Manager and
joined Nettie in trying to bring a new lease on life to the
boarding-house business. After some papering, painting and re-
furbishing of dining room, kitchen, halls, and bedrooms, and a
little modest advertising, they hoped for the success of this essentially new venture.

Their hopes were to be realized; they were destined to keep a
very fine establishment. If anything tended to mar the general
community atmosphere, it was the competitive jealousy of Mrs.
Ella Banks, who also took occasional boarders next door in the
Warren house, once a noted tavern.

As it transpired, the arrival of Mr. Patten, a total stranger, was
what helped John and Nettie most in beginning a long period
of success and pleasant congeniality. Mr. Patten came from
"down country", as we would have said then. He had read of a
summer boarding-house here, and it sounded so good to him that
he decided to take a chance on it and came without communicating ahead.

From Philadelphia, and changing trains in New York, he got
on one which, according to directions in the leaflet, would bring
him to Bellows Falls, Vermont. There he found the Alstead Stage,
an early "Autocar" driven by Len Bragg, and on it he rode to
Papermill Village. Here he met the driver of the one-horse stage
for East Alstead and Marlow. This man, when asked about the

boarding-house, said that yes, he knew an excellent one; although it did not have a cupola or a long porch, still it was just the place to spend the summer. Mr. Patten got in.

After a five-mile ride they reached the top of the hill in Mill Hollow, and turned into the yard of the big white house of the very prim and proper Ella L. Banks.

Now it seemed that when Mr. Patten had a summer's vacation, he liked complete relaxation from the formal requirements of city life; he discarded neckties, let his shirt collars go unbuttoned, his pants unpressed, his shoes unpolished, and did not shave. So when Mrs. Banks answered his knock, she remained inside the locked screened door. From this cool vantage point she suspiciously surveyed from head to foot the total aspect of this unknown, unheralded, unkempt character now two or three days along on his vacation practices. She said, "I don't have any room."

When the waiting driver, Clinton J. Gates, was told this— when it came to boarding-houses he was in the Ella Banks camp —he said that in that case he would take his passenger to another good place (kept by one of Ella's relations) only about a mile ahead on his route, and they started off. He whipped up his horse to a fast trot, and after about a hundred yards they sped past a big green house with a cupola and a long porch. Mr. Patten did not have much time to scrutinize it, but he shouted to the driver that must be the place he had in mind. "Oh, you wouldn't want to stay there," Mr. Gates said, urging the horse on at full speed. "You wait till you see the place I'm going to show you." Mr. Patten gave up—for the moment.

Reaching the East Alstead "common," they changed mail bags at Sarah J. Fish's brick store and post office, and started on up the hill beyond. The driver pointed up ahead to the Partridge house at the top of the hill and said, "There it is!" After one look, Mr. Patten, finally convinced he was being deliberately deceived, said, "No, I will not go there!" and demanded to be let off.

With suitcases in hand, he started walking back.

At the Cupola House, with its long porch, bright green clapboards and white scalloped trim, "Nettie M." and John were not at first favorably impressed either. But somehow, after talking

with him a few minutes, they found him a pleasant and reasonably intelligent man. Then, too, since they were just starting in business, they needed their first boarder. That evening we learned of the other factors in his favor, when Johnnie came over to tell us that at last they had their first patron. After describing their first doubts, Johnnie said, "But he seems all right. He says he is some sort of a teacher. And he even offered to pay us for a month in advance; you realize we charge $12.00 a week, so he must be somebody." He expressed the fervent hope that he and Nettie had not made a grievous mistake. It just so happened that my mother and stepfather had heard of this man and were able to assure Johnnie that they would not regret their decision.

And so it proved.

Mr. Patten at once became a "star boarder." Through many seasons to follow, their success and most desirable patronage came about largely through his influence.

Not just a "tourist," bent on luxury, leisure, and ostentatious indulgence, he was interested in culture, the local community, and the countryside, exploring all its old roads, paths, and hilltops. He often conducted other visitors on walking tours.

When he would go on some of his contemplative walks alone, though stoop-shouldered, he strode along as if with a purpose, always with cane or staff—sometimes with a hoe after heavy rains, as one of his hobbies was draining puddles in the road, of which we had plenty in those days!

Mr. Patten was an easily discernible figure from a distance. One or two summers he rode a pony. The pony was so small and Patten's legs were so long that his feet hung ludicrously close to the ground; the hunched-over rider and his mount together presented a most unsophisticated aspect—and it was unmistakably him all right! On the pond, in one of the old flat-bottomed punts common in those days, he found that with so many strokes of a canoe paddle on the left and then the same number on the right—the cycle repeated continuously—he could hold to an almost straight course indefinitely, as he once thus described his theory and practice to my father when they met down at the shore.

Mr. Patten often attended the serious discussions which my parents held, up in the "hall" on the second floor of our old mill (rebuilt) where we had a big fireplace and lots of chairs.

At one of these gatherings, attended by people full of earnest questions and concern, the subject was the institution of marriage. I was sitting next to Mr. Patten when the discussion started. During one of the pauses inevitable at the start of such a subject, I undertook a disarming but—as it proved—misconceived pleasantry. Perhaps seventeen at the time, and with a lack of discretion as to the time and place for levity, I said to him, "Well, Mr. Patten, since you and I are not married, we had better just keep still and listen to others, don't you think?"

"Perhaps we should," he answered in a very subdued tone, and he said nothing more. The same night, after we got back to the house, my mother gave me the very dickens: "That was a terrible thing you said; you must never make such fresh remarks to people whose lives you know nothing about. . . . That woman who spent a few days with us recently at the cabin was his divorced wife."

At another gathering, the "land question" was brought up. My parents were always hot on that subject! Mr. Patten had lived in Iowa in his youth and knew first hand what life was like out there in the 1860's and 70's during the great settlement boom days. Later he had studied these things academically in his mature years. He was not taken in by the critical opinions of the first midwestern settlers who looked with disdain on the poverty and "shiftlessness" of subsequent waves of immigrants. What he contributed to this discussion was the realization that the first settlers had pre-empted all the best lands. Submarginal natural opportunities and inferior competitive potentialities were all that were left for the late comers, except at speculative prices demanded by those who had got there first.

On one of Mr. Patten's frequent, contemplative walks by the road around the pond one of his "plates"—discarded for comfort, I should say, rather than for informality!—fell through a hole in his coat pocket, not to be missed until dinner that evening. But young Ted Spurr, always ready to oblige, especially for easy money, started right out to retrace the route. He found and returned the lost article to a most grateful owner, and collected a twenty-dollar reward.

And who was this man—this stranger appearing in our midst in 1910. unannounced, unprepossessing in the extreme, unknown except indirectly by my parents—who stayed for the last eleven summers of his life, to become respected by all, with a unique place of his own in the community?

He was *Simon Nelson Patten*, A.M., Ph.D., LL.D. (1852-1922). He was born on a farm in Iowa and later became principal and superintendent of public schools there and in Illinois; educated at universities in Europe and the United States; author of twelve books on economic and social philosophy; internationally known economist; writer of folklore, verses, and a novel; professor of political economy from 1888 to 1917 at the University of Pennsylvania.

The Last Word

As a docile child I had often felt under the domination of a very pious and nosey aunt, a frequent visitor at our house. A Seventh Day adventist fundamentalist, she was a lifelong, thorough, but opportunistic student of the Bible. Being, myself, anything but that, I could never have questioned her pronouncements, inferred from that age-old source, either about the future of humanity or the proper conduct of our family's personal attitudes or affairs. (For us she was very much a Harriet Livermore, that "not unfeared, half-welcome guest" described in Whittier's *Snowbound*.) From childhood into young manhood, there lurked in me the smoldering desire to beat her at something, just anything, to get even for once, or just to show that it could be done, if indeed that were possible.

At last—after ten to fifteen years of biding my time—a positively golden opportunity seemed "at hand".

While calling on my father during one of her stays of several days at his house, I sat in on one of her earnest and critical dissertations. This included a very mean and scathing judgment about someone then the object of her scorn, after which she turned to me and said, "Don't you agree with me, Heman?"

"Oh, Glory Be!", I thought to myself. "This is what I have waited for for years!" It seemed too good to be true, but I leaped into the situation with high expectations of pious revenge.

With every ounce of superior righteousness I could display— and with my father, long a submissive victim of her officiousness, looking on—I said, with triumphant pride and clarity, "No, Aunt Edith, I shall obey the Bible, which says, 'Judge not!' "

But alas, her swift comeback taught me, once and for all, never to tangle with anyone in a field he has made specially his own—

41

a lesson I have never forgotten since that dark day of my misconceived reprisal.

She was ordained, so it seems, always and forever to have the last word. She said, "Ah! but it also says, 'Judge rightly that ye shall know the truth!'"

Rare Species Identified

ONE OF OUR NEIGHBORS, Artemus Brubaker, who long ago departed our community, had left the general vicinity of Boston in search of a better life about the same time my parents had made the same move. He quit a region which he and they thereafter always referred to as "The Hellpot," and which, for him, was associated with bitter memories of a shattered home life and business career. Life here was a new outlet for his physical, mental, and creative gifts, his education and his great sense of humor, for the few years he was here.

One day, when he heard that I was going to Bellows Falls in my old home-remodeled Model T truck, he asked me to go to the railroad freight office to see if anything had come for him. We were always doing such services for each other.

Entering that office, I saw at the desk an old man I had never seen there before.

On my stating my errand, the old freight agent seemed startled as he turned sharply, wide-eyed, toward me and said, "Anything for. . . . what was that name again?"

"Artemus Brubaker," I repeated clearly.

Then he repeated the name several times, almost in a whisper; evidently it was calling up some long-lost but significant memory. In his swivel chair he turned pensively toward the bright afternoon sun shining through the open door that gave access to the platform and side-tracks. After a long moment of deep thought, he suddenly came to life, swung quickly around, and with a look of triumph, exclaimed, "By God! That was him!"

Though I could not possibly have known it until he got through reveling in his choice and long-dormant recollection,

what he was thinking of was an event in the earlier life of Artemus, well publicized at the time, which I, too, had not thought
of for many years.

It all started when he began planning a suburban house for a
Mr. and Mrs. Walker. Mrs. Walker, by far the more dynamic
and imaginative of that couple regarding household matters, was
the one who represented them during the constant consultations,
and Artemus found her a most congenial client; in fact, both he
and Mrs. Brubaker came to enjoy a very warm friendship with
both the Walkers for two or three years. But, unfortunately,
this pleasant, mutual relationship subsided when Mrs. Brubaker
became suspicious of the propriety of her husband's attentions
to Mrs. Walker. A strain arose over this which finally became
intolerable. In the end Artemus found himself the defendant in
a dramatic divorce proceeding, and destined, at its outcome, to
lose his home and children—and some old friends. But happily
he gained the renewed respect and support of others; my father
was among these, taking an understanding interest in Artemus
and later helping to preserve the memory of the case.

Even up to that time Artemus would have been too keen an
observer of public life to have taken at face value the usual run
of legal jurisprudence or other political institutions; but when
all the shenanigans in this case were over, he was to retain an
even more acute and lifelong contempt for most lawyers, all
courts, newspapers, and schemers of all kinds.

In court, in the case instituted against him, he took the stand
in his own behalf. But as he glanced over the crowded room,
he felt—as he had in the preceding weeks—the utter hopelessness of making his true position clear. Plainly, he was to lose
the unequal struggle; but he had long resolved, come what
might, that he would remain loyal to his own inner lights. In
response to any questions that might be put to him, there
would be no recriminations on his part. There would be no
backward looks; he would look steadfastly ahead, get through
with this dismal business as decently and quickly as possible.

While thus inwardly fortified, he was approached during
cross-examination by his wife's attorney, who, in a voice heard
clearly by court, jury, public, and press, said, "Uh . . . will
you please explain to the court just what there is between you
and this other woman?"

44

After a moment's thought, in a quiet voice Artemus said, "We feel drawn to each other, that's all."

Now here was a choice and unexpected break for the attorney, the chance to regale his audience, at Artemus's expense, with the seeming discovery of a rare phenomenon then in popular verbiage. Pursuing it with obvious relish, he said, "I see . . . very interesting." Then drawing closer and in an oily tone, he deliberately asked his last question: "Uh, Mr. Brubaker, could it possibly be that you two are soulmates?"

What an inane term! Artemus must have thought.

But by this time he would not risk a moment's delay in the termination of these shabby proceedings by arguing over the fine points of any such catchword of the day; better to let this obnoxious examiner think to have it his way in any such irrelevant or cheap attempts at humorous conjecture.

"Perhaps that's it," in a completely noncommittal tone, was all he said.

A simple answer, but, Oh! what grist for the press!

I was only a little boy at the time; in whatever my parents may have read of the case then I would have been just as oblivious to the human tragedy of it as Whittier's "Robins that sang in the orchard . . ."

But now, as a grown man, standing in the office of the old freight agent, I must have looked utterly puzzled by his exclamations.

"Artemus Brubaker!" he said again, almost as if to himself, marveling at this unexpected resurrection of an event long buried in the past. "Yes, sir, that was him all right! . . . By God, I ain't thought of that for years! . . . Read all about it when it happened . . . That was the name all right . . . Couldn't o' been no other."

Finally, turning to me, he explained: "Before your time, I guess . . . Most thirty years ago it was. . . . Down to Boston they found a couple o' soulmates. He was one of 'em!"

Whose Business Was It?

I RECALL a bright spring morning in 1936, when, along with many others caught up in the general excitement, we were going down to Alstead Village to see the effects of the spring flood. Warren's Brook—the culprit in this story—paralleled our road and passed under the bridge on the Acworth Road not 100 feet north of the junction of the two roads. Here we met Rol Hamlin, whose house stood just south of this junction. From his very first words we saw that he was in an angry mood. He had been trying all morning to get the State Highway Department on the phone to demand restitution of some sort for the water in his cellar.

I asked him to explain what had happened.

"Well, you see, the anchor ice built up so high under the Acworth Road bridge, right there," he said, as he pointed that way, "that when the flood got started, the brook water couldn't get under the bridge, so it ponded up above the bridge, came right over the road where we stand and down on to my property and filled my cellar. I'm pretty Goddamn sore about it!"

"Did the road men realize what was happening?" I asked.

"I don't know if they did or they didn't," he said.

"How long was the ice building up?" I asked.

"Oh, for two or three months, but much worse just lately."

"You knew all about the situation for some time then, didn't you?" I said. "You must have realized it could be dangerous."

"Well, I guess I did!"

"Why didn't you tell the road men or the Highway Department?"

"Who me? Why, hell, it wa'n't none of my business!"

46

Parish Council Meeting

ONE MINISTER of the Gospel who served our community for several years came to be regarded as radical in his political outlook, too unconventional in his concept of how best to plan and direct the work of the four churches "yoked" together in our Larger Parish. In regard to some bitter questions that arose, he was too independent in word and deed, as it proved, where more humility and cooperation with deacons, trustees, and parish council might have brought needed wisdom to bear.

By the time he left the parish, church members were deeply divided into those who revered him and those who reviled him, with much unnecessary misunderstanding between them and with very few taking any intermediate ground or dispassionate view of the matter as a whole.

Reports of the whole situation—and it was indeed a "situation"!—were naturally confusing to those in the State Conference Office at Concord who were now asked to help us find our next pastor. Therefore, as a preliminary step they sent over a Mr. Chase (no relation to me) to "survey" the parish, its peculiarities, and its needs. A special meeting of the Parish Council was called in order to hear, discuss, and —so it was hoped—find answers for his questions and ours.

After being introduced, Mr. Chase said, "For a long time, conflicting reports have reached our office regarding your former pastor. I wish we might begin by your giving me a clearer concept of the man."

Prolonged and stony silence followed this very reasonable approach. So I, a veteran former chairman of the Council during many stormy sessions in the past year or more, said cautiously,

47

"Well, Mr. Chase, I think all will agree that he became a very controversial figure."

This aroused the wrath of one of our pastor's most devoted followers, who quickly rose, turned on me, and, pointing a trembling finger, said, with utmost scorn, "In *your* opinion!"

Planned Economy

THE DOWNING PLACE had once been quite an establishment—a large farm for its day—with sheep and cattle, pastures and mowings, a maple sugar house, sugar lot and woodlot, and—half a mile down the river—a water-powered sawmill. But in the past thirty years or so the road passing the place had changed. From just a town road of dirt and mud, used mostly by neighbors teams, it had become a busy black-topped thoroughfare, on which there whisked past an alien and oblivious world. In the meantime, the life of the old place shrank down to a minimum of household activities of a quiet and aged pair—the last of the Downings—Ellen and her brother Herbert.

Herbert never spoke; he had been mute from birth. Now he was the docile object of Ellen's loving care, and she helped him dress, directed him at meals and bedtime, and throughout the day told him which of the few simple chores to do next. She probably gained much psychic support from always consulting him on matters that a man on a farm would naturally manage, but—getting no response—of course, would then always follow her own judgment.

Early one fall, a kind neighbor decided it would be too much for Herbert this year to saw up the Downings' winter's wood—as he had always done, by hand with a bucksaw. So the neighbor hired me with my portable engine and saw rig and two helpers to come and do the work all up at once.

One clear, cold day in late October we came to the Downing Place. We maneuvered the saw rig into position beside a long pile of four-foot wood, convenient for sawing and throwing into the open shed. But as we were about to start up the engine, a question arose regarding the cord or so of dry wood already in the back of the shed. So I went into the house to ask.

As I entered the kitchen—always the most active room in any New England farm house—Ellen was sitting in the sun by the window, watching operations at the shed across the driveway; Herbert was at the sink on the north side of the room wiping dishes. As I spoke to the two old people, she alone responded, but with a lively nod and friendly greeting. It was evident to me, who had never seen them before, that she was the one to be consulted, so I said, "Miss Downing, what about that dry wood

in the back of the shed? Wouldn't you like it piled by the door to use first?"

"Well, I'll have to ask Herbert about that," she said, and, facing about, called, "Herbert! Herbert, you come here."

Slowly he turned, and, with plate and towel in hand, shuffled in felt slippers over to stand by her side, where she took his arm, gently pulled him closer and drew his head down to her and shouted in his ear, "Herbert, Mr. Chase wants to know what to do with the old wood at the back of the shed. You want it saved out?"

He gazed down at her; gradually he turned his benevolent eyes in my direction, then slowly looked to her once more. No sound from him, no visible reply of any kind could have been detected by a waiting world in that long moment of respectful silence and close attention.

Finally, as his gaze turned toward the floor, Ellen looked up to me, and with a nervous jaw and blinking eyes, said, "I think Herbert has a plan about that wood: he'll use it just 's it comes."

Sex Education

ENLIGHTENING the young regarding the origin of babies and all other related "facts of life" used to be an almost universally avoided matter in the country where I grew up. Probably it still largely is. But now, forty years after the event to be here related, living in a more fragmented community, and moving oftener among those who today, thank God, have gained a more practical, sane, realistic, and humane attitude toward the life and problems of childhood, I cannot accurately judge just what progress may have been made by "the general". Some, I am sure.

Anyhow, in the days of my youth, for most parents the urgent necessity to think fast as to how to suppress or otherwise side-step the children's questions, whenever or in what unexpected form these might come, would be met with whatever degree of crudity or finesse had, up to the moment, characterized the relations of parents and their children. Of course, many common adult attitudes and conversations confused and aggrevated the social atmosphere for the young then—just as now the hypocrisy of the adult cocktail set confuses or offends the best in our youth of today. When a soldier from Marlow was reported killed in France in 1917 my first reaction was to say that it served him right for my embarrassment, suffered eight or ten years before, by his sly trick of having urged me to ask my Alstead Center teacher what a certain common four-letter word meant, even though afterwards she and my parents—with surprising aplomb! —had cheerfully counseled forgetting it.

On the occasion in question, during a warm, bright summer day, half a dozen men, who had volunteered to help rebuild the recently burned-out farm homestead of old Jack Rattigan and his wife Gurtie, were eating lunch, lying around on the pasture grass across the road in the shade of the old maples, and, as usual, joined by old Jack himself. One of the men, in whose family some child had probably created a recent, embarrassing situation, brought up the subject with his question: "What in hell can you say when your kid asks where he come from?"

After some others had made a few leering remarks, old Jack leaned forward, and with the stern and self-assured tone of finality with which he always stated "what's what" on all subjects, gave what was indeed accepted on this occasion as a sufficient, irrefutable, and final answer to this age-old and annoying sort of question.

"Well, I'll tell you fellows what I done", he said. "When my youngest boy asked us that, I yanked him right up from the supper table, and out in the shed I give him the God damnedest lickin' he ever had, and I says to him, I says, 'Don't you dare to ever ask no such question as that again!' . . . We never had no more trouble with him".

The Road Agent Question

THE ROADS of each small New Hampshire town have always been maintained by a "Road Agent" whose annual election was among the three most important contests in town meeting. To get over all the roads in town, summer and winter, spring and fall, and to the satisfaction of everybody, was a very tough job for any man.

After long and thoughtful consideration of the general layout of the roads of our town, my stepfather, Hartley Dennett, conceived the idea that the care of the roads could more economically be entrusted to two road agents instead of one. In the earnest but diffident manner he always had in all public affairs and gatherings, he presented his idea in town meeting, and made an appropriate motion, which was seconded.

Whatever important disadvantages of the proposition were advanced during the ensuing discussion, I do not recall, but when finally put to a vote, the motion was defeated.

Still convinced of the validity of our having two road agents, the following year Hartley repeated his proposition—for the last time as it proved—again making the same motion as before. The motion was duly seconded, and the moderator said, "Is there any discussion?"

John Allen, lifelong resident and caustic wit, was sitting on the back bench beside his old friend, the then perennial incumbent to the office in question. Still in his bearskin coat, he rose to his feet, was given the floor by the moderator, cleared his throat, to settle the question forever, and brought down the house with his one remark: "I should say, one road agent is bad enough."

A Use for Education

HARRY CRAIG was the youngest member of a large farm family, and had always lived on the place where he was born. He never married. The last years of his short life—he died at thirty-three in a sawdust pile cave-in—were spent with his brother and sister-in-law. He helped with the chores and all the other work on the place—caring for the cattle, woodcutting, sugaring, haying, potato digging, corn cutting, snow shoveling; in fact, all the regular jobs to be done on a northern New England farm on a wind-swept hill.

But Harry often had time for odd jobs as well, for neighbors and summer people. He was always cheerful, entertaining, and capable at cutting brush, digging ditches, carpentry, and the like. He was humorous, kindhearted, and accommodating. I should add that he was compassionate, too; digging a ditch for me one day in the late fall, he left one section of ground undisturbed, but had tunneled under it. When I asked him about it, he said, "I saw that a chipmunk had a hole there, and he was bringing nuts to it. I just couldn't bear to destroy his home and winter storehouse."

Early one summer, one of our most illustrious summer neighbors was distressed to see how the growth of trees in her hedgerow was blocking off her view of the pond. She asked Harry if he would cut away some of the wood and brush to open up the view. He said he would.

"Now, Harry," she said, "how much would you charge me?"

He told her $3.60 a day. (That was the regular charge in our part of the country in those days for what is called—somewhat erroneously—"unskilled labor.")

"Oh, Harry! I couldn't pay you that! . . . But I'd pay you $3.00 a day . . . Will you do the work, Harry?"

"Oh, yes, I'll do it," he said, good-naturedly giving her the satisfaction of settling the terms.

"But I'll tell you, Heman," he said to me, ending the humorous recollection with a word as to how he had not, in the end, been imposed upon, "I didn't go to school for nothing. I know how to figure a three-dollar day!"

Edna

(1878 - 1956)

THE LATE MARION NICHOLL RAWSON was one of our most illustrious neighbors. Brought up in New Jersey, she had married John A. Rawson, son of a local farm family. Since he was a college teacher, we saw them mainly as "summer people." She survived him by thirty years or so but continued here summers the rest of her life. She preferred generally to be called Marion, but I was among the few permitted to call her Edna, so Edna she will always remain for me.

Her little house here, halfway from Mill Hollow to East Alstead and adjoining the cemetery lot given the town by John's grandfather, was a veritable museum of early American household things, reflecting her lifelong status as a devoted and thorough antiquarian. In this field she was a lecturer and writer, having published by 1942 twelve books on such subjects as little old village mills, furniture, farm tools, household utensils, and so on, including what is the nearest thing ever written as a history of our town, and another book—*Candle Days*—whose title I mention as it best epitomizes the age of greatest interest to her. All her works were illustrated by her deftly made pen-and-ink drawings and sketches. She also made many water-color paintings of local places, including one of my millpond and blacksmith shop, a much prized memorial to her devotion to our community. Her house was (as it still is) a reflection of her own character, fireplace, low ceilings, plaster walls woodwork aged a natural brown, ornate cast-iron kitchen stove and schoolhouse stove—the only sources of heat in the house—all so appropriate to her. Likewise was the old-fashioned, two-hole "backhouse" attached to the ell; the water supply, hoisted by buckets from an old well in the yard; and the attached little barn housing her collection of old farm tools, flax wheels, spinning wheels, and the like. Edna never had a telephone, but reluctantly had electric lights her last few years.

In the field of historical writing, Edna was the subject of much discussion locally and some disagreement. This sprang from her famous book, *New Hampshire Borns a Town*, which purported to be the history of just any typical town in our state, but was actually of ours, giving real names of people and vicinities but mentioning only "The Town." Some appreciated her imaginative style, while others were critical of her lack of documentation and occasional flights of fancy and flowery verbiage. She was given to statements that people *"always"* did something in some certain way, while your own experience, wisdom, or study taught you that there were in fact usually many ways. She was not an expert on mechanical design and arrangement; her drawings were often excellent, and even explicit, but their "sketchiness" sometimes saved her from error—more than can be said of some of our more famous historians of early American life!

When our Historical Society was considering candidates to write an official history of the town, one member said, with much feeling, "I would not favor Mrs. Rawson for this; she is more romantic than accurate." And at that time I supported his view. I, too, had thought she composed many of her concepts of our town's past, dressing up the known facts with too many of her own imaginings.

I remember, for example, her vivid description of one of our most noted first settlers, Nathaniel Sartel Prentice, who settled here in 1774 on a hilltop farm, later became famous in Revolutionary times and in church, town, and state affairs. Our Society had accompanied Edna up the hill to the old Prentice farmstead with its cellar hole, stoned-up well, scattered barn foundation stones, and Nathaniel's orchard's scrawny progeny. As we stood about the cellar hole, upon the curly, gray, pasture grass then yielding to the encroaching hardhack and returning pine forest, Edna described Nathaniel and Martha Prentice's life and times. Pointing toward the old lane up which we had just hiked and which had once been a route of the early stagecoaches, she said, "Every day when the stage went by, no matter what

Nathaniel was doing, he always turned and waved to the driver."
I blush today at the lack of historical and human imagination I
then had which caused me, on that occasion, to say to myself,
"How does she know he did that? Why make up such stuff?"

But that was at least thirty-five years ago; in that time I began
to pay more attention to human nature and the principles of
historical facts and study, and to what literature can do for us.
I can now appreciate Edna as an historian of the people—in
contrast with works on the past giving us mainly only war and
politics. She invested the bare facts with the stuff of human life,
with what early life meant to the people themselves, reminding
her readers or listeners of what it was like, battling it out with
Nature and in such wind-swept or such forest-bound and remote
locations where they courageously put down roots—the Pren-
tices, for example. How did she know that "he waved to the
driver"? Why, country people under such circumstances have
always done such things! Maybe many of us knew that, as we
stood with her on that exact historic spot, but for her to have
embellished the recitation of the mere facts with gestures and
with visualizations of the settlers' undoubted inner feelings all
brought to us the sense of reality, the living breath of history
which so distinguished her writing and speaking.

Because neither Edna nor I were perfect, each with his own
brand of temperament, scheme of values, and ways of self-
expression, some little spark struck by chance contact caused
between us a general offishness that marred our great friendship for a while. I really do not know what actual incident
started this, but I find it pleasant to contemplate how Providence restored our normal good feelings—aided by the triviality
of the paltry sum of fifty cents!

Driving up to The Common at East Alstead, with my trailing
cord-wood saw rig, I stopped at Edna's to pay her for a secondhand battery, and handed her two dollars. "We agreed on two
dollars and fifty cents," she said. "Don't you try to put anything
over on me!" I responded with words and tone calculated to win
my contention; in the end I drove off in a huff, on up to The
Common to saw wood for a friend.

The October day with its gorgeous autumn foliage was most
enchanting; Willie had his brother and other congenial help on

59

hand; the wood was piled conveniently; the engine performed well; the belt stayed on—in fact, the day and the work were all so satisfactory as to cause a general elevation of spirits, the alleviation of any discordant feelings, the viewing of all life's little ups and downs in clear perspective. And the thought took shape: Why let fifty cents stand in the way of a long and rich friendship and the continued sharing of many of life's great values? On my way home, stopping at Edna's, I was greeted by more than passing friendliness as I extended the fifty cents and the acknowledgment that quite likely I had been wrong.

"Come in, I want to tell you about my afternoon," Edna said. "I walked up through the cemetery and then down through Grandpa Rawson's woods. The colored leaves were so beautiful, the bird songs so joyous, the air so still and peaceful that I suddenly thought how fortunate I was to live in such a place, and how I should never get upset by little matters—like a fifty-cent misunderstanding with you. I am sorry for what I said."

Then and there we ended our years of mutual suspicion, laying the foundation for a restored and solid friendship and the renewed sharing of knowledge and common interests. This was all appropriate to her very good mind, sincere Christianity and Quaker faith. I hope that I, too, may have gained something of added grace appropriate to my upbringing.

All in all, that October day was a landmark.

Everything considered, Edna's sayings, writings, and paintings are a unique and colorful legacy to our community, enriching the "inner life" of those who knew her and those who would search out the human substance of our past.

We often gained amusement—in which she would cheerfully join—from various of her traits, tastes, or mannerisms, two of which stand out for me now: her vehement preferences, and her picturesque slips-of-the-tongue.

Illustrative of the first:

Her devotion to the life and history of the people of America and of our town in particular was mostly on the colonial period (and that of but few following decades) and the works of the handicraft age. To her, events of the past century or more, and the products of the machine age, were unworthy of attention or tribute. On one occasion, a young tourist couple asked her about

60

the history of the well-known Cupola House in Mill Hollow. This had been built originally as a boardinghouse in 1865, elaborately trimmed with band saw work around 1900, and renewed as an excellent summer boardinghouse meticulously kept, during my boyhood. She told them: "Oh, it really has no history."

And of the second, I well recall what may seem a tiny but choice tidbit for those who relished catching her in seemingly telling slips.

As I was riding home from church with her one very sweltering Sunday, she noticed a scarecrow in a cornfield, quickly drove off the road, and reached for her sketchbook, saying, "Ah! For weeks I have been looking for a good scarecrow to draw!"

Fervently wishing to get home and go swimming, I said, "Why Edna, you could compose one at home just as good as that one."

"Heman Chase!" she said, "I'll have you know scarecrows are one thing I will not fake."

How Rumors Start

IN THE LATE AFTERNOON of a summer day in the haying season, we saw a huge column of brown smoke rising some distance to the north of the East Alstead Common. We started there at once.

All sorts of vehicles had been ditched along the roads converging at Craig's Corner, and men, women, and children with anxious faces were hurrying up to the tragic scene at the Craig farm.

All the farm buildings on that wind-swept hill, if not actually connecting, were too closely ranged for safety in such an event. By this time, the big barn at the north end, where a loaded hay truck had backfired on the barn floor—as we were told days later —was all a mass of flames and half-consumed, and from there the fire was already rushing down through the sheds to the big, four-square, Colonial-overhung-type farmhouse. Clearly, for the whole complex, the hours were numbered; we had no fire company then worthy of the name.

But friends did all they could. Carts, ox yokes, milk cans, tools and equipment of every description were dragged from the outbuildings as long as they could be approached. At the house, furniture, bedding, clothes, pictures—useful, old, or cherished things that rescuers could lay their hands on quickly—were carried out and across the road to safety under the old maples. In the front hall and stairway was a hurrying, stumbling mass of hard-breathing men—and a few women—crowding past each other heavily laden. There were shouts of "Gangway" and other admonitions and questions, and later glances toward the upper and northerly rooms as smoke and crackling flames began pouring in. If anyone had glimpsed the panel of quaint old murals above the fireplace, he must have quickly abandoned it for something movable. And, although there would have been time and opportunity to save it, in all the noisy confusion no one thought of the forty gallons of maple syrup in the cellar. At the end, a minute or so before the urgent, authoritative-sounding warnings for all to get out for the last time and stand clear, a neighbor and I, putting stones at its hinge-side jamb, closed and pried free the fine old seven-paneled front door—happily destined to center and grace the reconstruction a year or two later.

When nothing more could be done, we joined a few oldtimers watching gloomily from the west meadow.

Gene Wilder, in a reflective tone and for anyone that might be listening, recalled that he had once lived in that old house. He bewailed the sadness of its untimely end and the difficult times

ahead for the family. "God! It's too bad!" he said. "I don't know what they'll do." Later he said, "They'd ought to sell what they saved to an auction right away, folks'd bid like thunder." After a while old John Riordan came hobbling up on his peg leg; he and Gene greeted each other in sad tones, as we all gazed quietly at the gradual unfolding of this big old farmstead and its generous house, now revealing the hardwood framing of a past age and, for this last moment of its life, glorified by its stairway railings trimmed with shimmering gold.

After a time, but now in a natural and matter-of-fact tone of voice, Gene said, "Well, I always said, it don't pay to put green hay in the barn."

At once John murmured reflectively, "No, by God, it don't!"

We continued to watch, each of us with his own thoughts, the odd-angled, slowly settling profile of the old Craig Homestead as now and then a collapsing panel would open up a new view through to the horizon or a beam would fall with a muffled crash followed by a shower of sparks leaping with the flames high in the air. Or someone would tell what he had been doing when he first saw the smoke in the sky, or mutter the question in everyone's mind: "What'll they do?"

Finally, John clearly asked, "Is that what started it?"

"God! I don't know," Gene said.

The Case Taken to
a Higher Court

*"I shall have Ethan Allen hanged."—Governor of New York,
Albany, 1770.*
*"The Governor is forgetting a Natural Law: You can't hang
a man until you have first ketched him."—Ethan Allen, Ben-
nington.*

THE CITIZENS and public officials of a small town in Vermont were
long annoyed by what they considered the sly, underhanded,
and crooked actions of one of its residents. Let us assign the
name of Smith to this mean cuss. Smith's final offense was the
cutting of eighty dollars worth of timber on a woodlot owned
by the town. Backed by the citizens, the town's attorneys declared
this to be the last straw; it was time to take action. I was employed to survey the lot and make a map showing the cut-over
area, and otherwise prepare for court, where the attorneys swore
that at last they would get justice. They engaged a special trial
lawyer from fifty miles over the mountains to handle the case
when it should come to trial.

Visualizing the heavy expenses of this case looming ahead, I
asked the town's attorneys, "Do you really think that small
amount of timber worth a lawsuit?"

"Well, no, of course not," they said. And they explained that
Smith's recent offense was just one of a long series of such an-
noyances but was of such a nature that it gave them for the first
time a clean-cut chance to rock him back on his heels. Doing so
now might stop him. They had tried unsuccessfully to get
recompense from him by offering to stop the matter if he would
deed to the town his own small woodlot; it adjoined the town's
lot and was where he should have been cutting. He had said his wife

65

would never sign the deed. The attorneys were prepared for this evasion, and told him they had studied the records and found that his title was such that he could give a legal deed without her signature. Then it was that he got in the last word—a word on which the visit ended, as no rejoinder would have been possible or necessary: "That's true, but I have to live with her."

So they said they would take him to court. I happened to ask why they had engaged that distant attorney, as they could surely have handled the case themselves. They said: "He puts on a great show." How I looked forward to that! But, alas, we were all doomed to disappointment; Smith had the last move. Carrying perversity to new heights of defensive retaliation, he foiled the avengers of his depredations by his final stratagem: He died one week before the day set for trial.

A Great Show

WITH THE APPROACH of the date set for the case of Krogustinio vs. Kratrinski, I looked forward to their day in court with keen anticipation.

I had heard that Attorney Casper had been engaged by the defendant and that in the courtroom he could put on "a great show." My client, Mr. Krogustinio, had engaged Attorney Swift, who, for his overflowing wit and humor, was also well known.

Altogether, the forthcoming battle of tactics and brains promised to be memorable.

We were not disappointed.

The high point of the day—for those who had learned to regard court proceedings as a "show," which they essentially are—resulted from Attorney Swift's ill-fated attempt to undermine the "public image" of defendant Kratrinski. While in direct examination of his client, he asked, in a clear voice that all in the room might hear, exactly what occurred on a certain evening when he and Mrs. Krogustinio had met the Kratrinskis in front of the moving picture theatre.

"Mrs. Kratrinski spit at my wife," Mr. Krogustinio told the court. (This lawsuit involved the few inches by which, according to my survey, a small garage encroached on adjoining property.)

Then Attorney Swift pursued the matter of that event further, endeavoring, of course, to establish in the minds of the jury just what despicable characters the Kratrinskis were—certainly not to be believed in any testimony they might later give. Finally, when he evidently felt he had accomplished his purpose, he stopped, turned toward Attorney Casper and said, in the usual manner of inviting his opponent to cross-examine the witness, "You may inquire."

And, indeed, Attorney Casper did "inquire!" He continued at once the very same line of questioning already initiated by Attorney Swift, examining every detail of that outrageous act committed on the designated evening long ago, drawing Mr. Krogustinio out on every imaginable ramification not previously mentioned. One gained the impression that with his keen and fertile mind he could have carried this on indefinitely if need be.

But, as Attorney Casper had evidently rightly anticipated, Attorney Swift, in the way attorneys have of ostentatiously making an eloquent show of defending the court against the schemes of others in their own profession, suddenly stood up and said, "Your Honor, I object to this disgusting line of questions. It is irrelevant, immaterial, and an insult to the dignity and intelligence of this entire assemblage."

Attorney Casper's trick had worked; even before the court could rule on the admissibility of the objection, he had drawn himself up to full stature, and, by one clear, brief, final question, "brought down the house" all over the head of his Brother Attorney: "And who brought up this matter of spitting?"

A Lost Bet

MY HELPER, Ralph Forristall, and I were surveying around the boundaries of a large Vermont woodlot, and when we reached a point overlooking the farmstead of Harry Burton, it was almost time to begin thinking about lunch. The day being windy and raw, Ralph, who lived near there and knew everybody, said, "Let's go down and eat in Harry's house and get warm. He'll be glad to have us."

Indeed, this proved true.

After the greetings, Harry went to the kitchen and we took easy chairs in the corners of the living room and got out our sandwiches. Soon Harry returned with a big kettle of baked beans left for him on the back of the stove by Mrs. Burton before she had left for town. As he set the kettle on the table, he said, "Now, gentlemen, no need to eat cold sandwiches today. Just come up and take chairs and join me in a good hot mess o' beans." He was very insistent, so we gave in—without much argument, the day being what it was.

When we got through, warm and much revived, I said, "Mr. Burton, thanks for those good hot beans; it was very good of you to treat us so generously, thank you so much."

"That's all right," he said. "But now I'll tell you something: I never do anything like that without expecting something in return. I want you and Ralph to give me just a little of your valuable time to help settle a small bet I have made. I have bet that the direction of a short piece of wall down in my woods, if extended, would show my back line up in the meadows."

I said that of course we would be glad to run that line.

After getting my compass where we had left off on our job, we went down in the woods and were shown the wall. From its north end we extended the line by a few set-ups of the compass. My last set-up was at the foot of a bank; Harry had run up ahead, and, standing at the top of the bank, called, "Just line me up." After I had done so, we saw him pick up a long branch, sight back and forth along it, himself thus undertaking to extend the line, in a very rough way, out into the open land beyond. Then he shouted back down the bank to us, "That's all, fellows! You've earnt your dinner! You can go!"

I picked up the compass and started off through the woods toward our job. But Ralph, his curiousity now aroused, did not immediately follow but instead climbed to the top of the bank to see for himself what the results might have been. When he caught up with me several hundred yards beyond, he said, "I'll tell you why he was through with us so quick. That line was headed right straight for his buildings!"

One Way to Check Land Titles

FOR BUILDING the airport at Claremont, New Hampshire, the town's attorneys had purchased all tracts of land they thought would make up the entire area needed. I was employed to make a map of the outer boundaries of the whole.

One day while watching bulldozers grading the field, obliterating all the old walls, fences and other landmarks, I felt a tap on the shoulder, and turning, faced a short, anxious, diffident little man who asked, "You the boss here?"

"No," I said, "but what can I do for you?"

Waving toward the machines, he said, "They cover up my land!"

"Just where is your land?", I asked.

With the former individuality of component parts of the field now hopelessly obscured, all he could say was that his land had been somewhere near where we stood. But then he pulled from his pocket a crumpled and soiled piece of paper to show me. This proved to be an informally written "agreement to sell." Actually it was a receipt for this man's payment of $100 toward the purchase price of a piece of land—presumably near here—with a stipulation that, after a second payment of the same amount, the owner would execute a formal deed of the land to this prospective purchaser.

So it did appear that this little man had some legitimate claim. I advised him to take it up with the town's attorneys.

Soon the attorneys telephoned and asked me to check the records in Newport to see if indeed the present owner of the land in question did have a good and saleable title. Because of the vast number of lands the owner appeared to have, the loss of landmarks on the airport, and the indefiniteness of descriptions

71

of land, the records were simply of little or no help. So I called on this owner.

He proved a paragon of candor. He said, "I inherited, and I have bought and sold so many pieces of land that sometimes I really am not sure in a given case. I think I own the lot you speak of I have found that often the best I can do to be sure of my title is to go ahead and sell it and see what happens."

A Judgment Regretted

IF WE COULD BUT LEARN to anticipate the lessons that retrospect may bring, we might in many human situations avoid eventual remorse by restraining the frequent impulse to ridicule or harshly criticize, wisely content to leave to the Creator the judgment of other men.

One bleak and snowy day in early winter, my rodman and I drove north a few miles along a main road traversing a most beautiful valley having high mountain ranges on either side. Then, turning east, we started up a side road that wound its way steeply up a western slope. Through the season's first accumulation of snow, but thanks to "four-wheel drive", we shortly made the climb of a mile or so, then turned off north along the old Hill Road, which with but gentle grades ran along the western side of the mountain. For a mile or more we passed scrub woods, brushy fields and pastures extending from the valley far below to the precipitous cliffs far above. Along the way there were numerous cellar holes and two tiny family graveyards, all reminders of an earlier day of teeming rural life long gone. Finally, far ahead there came into view the house and barns of the last place on the road to be run as a farm—that of Henry Corrigan.

Henry's grandparents had been among those Irish immigrants to America who—escaping old-world oppression and want—were willing to do the hard and monotonous tasks of construction and other basic or extractive industries of a new and growing country. Lumbering had been the mainstay of the economy of this particular vicinity. Like other refugees from the British Isles in the nineteenth century, the old Corrigans found land of their own relatively easy to get so that subsistence farming could supple-

73

ment money wages. Henry's father worked in the great lumber camps for many years, but when that business began to wane due to the depletion of the forests, he then attended more exclusively to farming.

On the death of his parents, Henry inherited the family farm. He kept cows and sold milk and young stock; he did trucking and other odd jobs for neighbors and summer people. Reports about how good a farmer he was and about other features of his life differed greatly. He did live alone, but, as I was to see, in a manner no more disorderly than most bachelors in similar circumstances. But his own lack of inner resources; the abandonment of the region by all his old neighbors; his own poor health and lack of ambition; and finally, the "cost-price squeeze" and other adversities then overtaking most small farmers, all combined to break him down. To sell out and move away was the only possible release in his case, and he had the place listed for sale. It was not long before he had a prospective buyer.

In the late 1930's Mark Langer came to America, went into a technical business in New York, taking up residence in one of the suburbs. Life and work there, as well as under the crowded, tense and oppressive conditions in Germany, gave Mark a deep longing for some sense of peace and quiet, the feeling of freedom and space around him, and contact with Nature—land of his own! His eye must have brightened and his step quickened when he read in the real estate columns of the *New York Times:* FOR SALE: 500-ACRE FARM, WITH HOUSE, barns, OUTBUILDINGS; 30 ACRES OF TILLAGE; MOUNTAIN VIEW. Maybe, he thought, this was the answer to his dreams!

At the very earliest opportunity, he came up from the city and contacted the agent. As they started out to see this "500-Acre Farm" so-called, Mark was at once entranced by the beautiful unspoiled scenery: along the valley road between the mountain ranges, up the steep side-road, along the level stretch by fields and pastures, old cellar holes and family graveyards, and then the old farm where they turned in and where Mark was introduced to Henry Corrigan. What happened to Mark that day was well expressed by his words to me the following summer: "I tell you, Mr. Chase, from this porch where we stand now I took one long look out over that valley and fell in love with the place".

74

Other conversations further reinforced my early impression that on that first visit Mark and his wife had somehow also taken a shine to Henry himself, a feeling which, as far as I know and although the going at times was tough, remained with them always.

In the search for "land of his own", Mark ended it then and there. He said he would buy the place.

When they all went to arrange the details of the transaction, Henry's attorney, Jack Williams, said that under the circumstances the farm should be surveyed and the records consulted to determine just what lands and how much acreage now comprised the property so that a proper description could be written for the deed. He said he knew a surveyor he could get for the work.

And so on that raw late-November day without the slightest inkling that the engagement was to prove in any way memorable or unusual, we drove up the steep driveway to Henry's house and set the brakes in front of the ell kitchen door—the all-but-universal approach to a northern New England farmhouse.

Henry could see us coming a long way off, and indeed he was in the doorway as I stepped off the running board of my truck.

To my first words—"Good Morning. Mr. Corrigan?"—he abruptly said (although my name and professional designation were conspicuously lettered on the truck door) "Are you with any insurance company?" I firmly denied any such presumably subversive association, and as we gained the porch, I introduced myself and my rodman and stated our business. Then gruffly he said, "Oh yes. Come in."

We sat on cheap, rickety old kitchen chairs in the large barren, chilly room in the southwest corner of the house. Obviously this had always been the kitchen. In addition to considerable disorder, its general arrangement suggested that it never had been conveniently thought out for the essential living and daily work of the most important room in any farmhouse. Now it was probably less homey than ever. Henry had been brewing his coffee on a tiny electric hot plate on the floor under the table that stood by the south window. Here he would sit to eat and gaze down that lonely road. If there was a range or chunk stove heating the room I do not now recall it, but in any case we did no more than loosen our winter coats.

As we became acquainted during that first visit, gradually orienting our minds to the situation, the scene before us seemed to sum up the disheartening end of an era and a way of life—of the American people; of a particular farm and place; and of a family and its last survivor. The effect on Henry of his defeat, by all the slow inexorable forces of change, came out in his raised voice and anguished cry of desolation: "I can't stay here any more!"

What is referred to as "New England Farm Abandonment" is thought of, if at all, by most people as just a matter of statistics. But what it meant in the inner lives of the people affected is often disregarded. For some, of course, quitting the farm and going into some simpler more specialized and more lucrative job was an exquisite relief from bondage to hard, monotonous, low-paying toil—and in rural isolation. But for others there were the heart-felt feelings of a vague intangible defeat by an invisible enemy; the shattered dreams of dominion over one's

76

own destiny, work and life; the blasted hopes; the paralyzing uncertainties of the future; the sleepless nights of weeping; the dawning of stark reality with the coming of the day; and the hard, inevitable decisions. I had witnessed much of these feelings before.

What feelings predominated in Henry at this moment of his life we could not have fully known that day. Some measure of humility on my part and the sensing of humiliation on his combined to give me pause, for I do recall that only after a time and with much hesitation and tactful effort could I bring myself to suggest our taking up the matter at hand.

Scattered snow flakes whizzed past the rattling old window panes as I said, "Well, Mr. Corrigan, the weather having become what it now is, of course we can't do any actual surveying today. But Jack Williams said you could show us around the boundaries. Could you do that now?"

By this time Henry fully realized we were on the level—not "connected with any insurance company." He said, "I'll tell you. A few weeks ago I was in a smash-up. I wasn't hurt much, and I'm most all right now. Their company offered me a settlement, but if I work it right I think I can get more. So I ain't going to be seen walking no further than to your truck. Looks like it can go anywhere; you drive me around where I tell you and I'll show you all I can, setting right in your cab."

I realize now (and may have then) how nearly universal this attitude of Henry's is among people in all stations of life. But at the time, this incident—this scheming strategy in the accident case—was just the beginning of a long series of observations enhancing a growing feeling of disgust I came to have toward a man seemingly so small, so mean and so selfish. This attitude was destined to dominate my thoughts of Henry for the next twelve years.

Through the growing blanket of snow and driving sleet we made our way that day over the old farm and logging roads, the margins of fields, the old Hill Road, the steep, winding short-cut to the valley road far below; we had Henry point out, as I made notes and sketches, all the old lines of trees, walls, wire fences and the like where his land cornered or crossed the roads. We halted often and , sitting crowded in the cab listened as he

77

described, none-too-clearly, how the boundaries ran in places far out of sight but which he assured us we could find.

In the days to come we finally got it all in mind after much deed study and consultations with adjoining owners, agents and others. The actual work of surveying was essentially uneventful and routine, as such work goes on mountain-side farms. There were the usual walls built by the earliest settlers and the remains of wire fencing of a generation or two later. The shape of the farm and woodland had, however, many odd details (there were forty-one corners!) that became evident as the map, augmented by each day's work, gradually developed on paper. Completing it took me about ten evenings in my "tourist room".

We dropped in on Henry several times, but it did not improve my disposition at all, listening to his many sour harangues.

We were fortunate in completing the survey in the lowering dusk of the last day preceding the closing of the sale. By that time I knew we had not been around any such acreage as had been advertised.

After dinner I joined Jack Williams in his office to work on the map and description, while he in his inner room worked at deed study and writing.

After scaling the map, my suspicions were confirmed: Henry had only 213 acres! When I informed Jack, he said in consternation, "My God, that's a terrible come-down!. . . . Well we can't help it. We'll just have to finish up on that basis. I hope the sale can still go through."

Soon steps were heard in the stairway, the door opened and a haggard but pleasant man entered, put out his hand and said, "I am Mark Langer; I just came up from New York." I told him who I was; then, not to risk being the "bearer of the evil tidings," I suggested he go straight in to see Jack.

Later, when they both strolled out to the front office, Langer said, "I'm dead tired so I shall go straight to my hotel." But then he added words that lifted our spirits: "I am sure everything will work out somehow," and he left. We went back to our respective tasks.

But soon it was Jack's turn to announce more bad news of his own: re-reading one document revealed that in a twenty-acre woodlot, already included in my calculations, map and description, Henry had only a life interest, the fact making it unsalable. This reduced us to 193 acres. But the best we could do at this point was to finish up all papers on this new basis.

At a very late hour we separated for the night with the mutual hope that Mr. Langer's good nature and practical sense would take this last blow in stride.

At the appointed hour next morning, all parties to the deal were on hand, and Jack closeted them in the inner office, and all seemed to quiet down. I remained at a little corner table in the outer office where I alternated between gazing down on the busy main street of the town and chatting with Jack's very attractive secretary.

After a time raised voices were heard amid a couple of bursts of laughter a matter of amused curiosity to us on the outside —only to be dispelled by Mr. Langer who came out to "take a breather", closed the door, and cheerfully faced us.

Rubbing his hands together, he said, "Well, we're going to do business . . . When I mentioned the shortage of acreage, Henry said, 'Why Mark, you wouldn't know an acre of land if you saw it!' Of course I had to admit that was true. And then he said, 'You don't need to worry. You'll have land enough.' I had to admit that was true too. . . . But anyhow, I got them to take off five-hundred dollars, so everything is going through all right." With that he rejoined the others.

Soon there was a scraping of chairs and congenial voices as the doors opened and the parties to the transaction came out and shortly dispersed. All had gone well in the end.

It is not often that the good will of one party to a deal can make up for significant and proven misrepresentation by the other. It stretches credulity to believe that Henry, having lived and worked all his life on that farm, could have made an "honest" mistake of 300 acres—150% in this case. And the 500-dollar rebate to Mark Langer was a mere token, considering the price of land at that time. (The agent, of course, could only have stated Henry's claim.)

Looking at this whole matter from Henry's side, the reader may formulate his own opinion. Mine is not yet fully resolved even to this day, for I know that in each successive era we are, in varying measure, as "chips upon the stream", living among the powerful forces of our times, the guilt or innocence of our yieldings rightly being left to the Creator's broader judgment.

In the next few years, on the long trips up to that region, I met Henry numerous times. His sour, cheerless and cynical remarks only reinforced my early disdain for his seeming dullness and insignificance. I had not even thought to ask others about him. His life seemed so devoid of use, meaning or purpose—lived so nearly for nothing—that when word finally came of the tragic ending of it, the fact simply did not seem like significant news.

But again, we must not be too ready to judge such matters. There may be so much that does not meet the eye. My being from another and distant town was, in this case, symbolic of all of us being far on the outside of others' lives, seeing dimly, if at all, what is inside. Several more years were to pass before I was to learn, with remorse, some of the things that were to compel a more restrained and compassionate view.

According to neighbors, for nearly all his adult years Henry had loved and courted Ellen Willard. She lived with her parents down in the little village in the valley below Henry's farm. Her brothers and sisters had long since left home, leaving Ellen with the increasingly arduous care of the old folks—bed ridden for years—and she attended them with selfless devotion. As long as she was needed, she felt she should not marry.

Henry became her devoted helper, moving to a nearby cottage after the sale of his farm, partly to be at hand during those times when a man is needed in sick-room situations. On the rare occasions when she could get away Ellen would take rides with Henry out into the country—for the good air, for companionship, for a respite from household tasks, and for private talks of hope-for things in a future of their own.

But one day, while Henry was at the Willards, Ellen began to complain of a great pain in her chest. At Henry's urging she went to the bathroom to take medicine of some sort and soon returned. Then, standing for a moment near Henry, she began to totter and sway, reached for his suddenly outstretched hand, and fell forward into his arms. In an instant he knew she was gone.

80

When the relatives came they removed old Mr. and Mrs. Willard to a nursing home and took charge of the property and all Ellen's affairs.

The events and conditions of Henry's life, I found—not surprisingly—gave rise to many differences of opinion, supporting the saying, "You can hear most anything in this town."

Many of the conflicting statements I heard:—whether he had been a good farmer; why he appeared poor, whether perhaps by lavishness on new cars, losses at the races or in the farm sale; whether he could sign a check or read a written letter; or whether he could read at all!—all seemed to indicate a sad lack of communication with other people. Certainly I was surprised on the day we first met that Henry could not—or evidently did not—read the word SURVEYOR emblazoned on my truck door at a time when he was so suspicious about our business.

After Ellen's death it was said by some that Henry, with nothing to live for, gradually became untidy and morose and just let himself go downhill. But others claimed he held up very well. He took a room for two years in a very pleasant and respecable home of friends of mine, partly for the very purpose of avoiding undesirable company, and they told me he had been quiet, kindly, clean and decent—in fact "a model guest".

Something of these better qualities seemed to have remained with him even to the last.

But all things considered, little imagination is needed to understand how, for Henry—"of all that made life sweet bereft" and most of the time in a state of at least partial psychic isolation— the road ahead looked, at best, dark, cold and lonely.

Finally he became caretaker for a big summer estate in a nearby town and was given comfortable quarters in one of the outbuildings. On one of the last days of the year a carpenter, who had been asked by the owners to do some interior work during the winter, went to the caretaker's house to discuss it. Henry, having arranged everything in a way obviously calculated to minimize the unavoidably disagreeable duties that would confront his discoverers, was found by the carpenter, two or three days "dead by his own hand."

81

Forever

A YOUNG COUPLE from New York were spending their vacation in Vermont at the girl's mother's place in the village of Grafton. They had planned to be married on this same trip. I happened to visit them there on the day they were to go to the local town clerk for the marriage license. Since I was well acquainted with both Mr. and Mrs. Cambridge, who together took care of the duties of the office, I offered to take my friends over and introduce them.

In the old brick house on the main street of the village, where the Cambridges lived, did much of their work, and kept the current papers and records, the couple sat at the table, facing Mrs. Cambridge as she wrote out the particulars. Mr. Cambridge and I, with nothing to do during this hushed interval, just stood idly around waiting while the work was done.

As I dwelt on the auspicious character of this moment in the young people's lives—with the hoped-for joys of companionship in the new relationship just beginning—the word "forever" came to mind.

With what turned out to be unacceptable levity—a weakness of mine not yet overcome in those days—I turned to Mr. Cambridge and said softly, " 'Forever' is a pretty long time, don't you think?"

Drawing himself up with an air of offended dignity and sense of propriety, he faced me and said, "No, young man, I don't agree with you at all. Mrs. Cambridge and I have been married thirty years and we are very happy."

Intoxication?

Late one October afternoon, I was starting home from Manchester, Vermont, filled with a sense of unusual satisfaction—perhaps even elation. Of course I am always glad, after some time away, to be heading back toward home and family. But there were special reasons this time.

The past few days I had had an interesting job on Mount Equinox, surveying the site of a dam and pond for Dr. J. G. Davidson, drawing preliminary plans and making estimates of volumes of earth and water; the prospects for more of that work in the future were good.

I had spent a night at the home of Walter and Margaret Hard, where after dinner we had passed the evening in Walter's study in stimulating and heartwarming conversations about literature, history, music, education, human nature, and other common interests and feelings about life. It was one of the earliest of many such occasions that came to enrich our friendship over the years.

Then, too, my old Ford pickup was performing with a spirit and energy not seen since it was new many years before, for I had just installed a freshly rebuilt engine, wartime lack of maintenance having up to then reduced the old one practically to junk.

So, on this happy day, car and driver were tearing along over my favorite mountains, full of forward spirits, around the winding turns and along the pleasant well-scraped surface of gravel and salted clay which State Route 11 then was.

The prospects for the pleasant and prosperous development of my work in this vicinity being what they were, it occurred to me that mileage records to various points along the way would be of future interest. I searched in the glove compartment for a notebook.

With no recollection whatever of the intervening time, space, or roadside obstructions, my next conscious moment was that of bouncing to a halt on the high bushy mounds and tussocks of a swampy pasture, unharmed but immobilized as it proved, silent and alone under the lowering sky. The road had curved sharply to the left.

My helplessness was evident at a glance. But with luck, possibly I might get help and get out before nightfall, I thought.

Up in the road, I walked easterly, past the Johnny Seesaw Ski Lodge, and on to the Best farm where I had often seen work horses. But the horses, it seemed, had just been put out to pasture for the night and the tenant farmer was in an uncooperative mood. I started back to the Lodge, and there Bill Parish, the thoughtful proprietor, generously offered me dinner, bed, breakfast, and towing arrangements for the next morning. He also drove me in his car to bring over my bags and valuables for the night.

Some distance further back toward Manchester, Fred Pabst was at that time beginning to build up the great ski development on Bromley Mountain.

In the morning as soon as Fred's caterpillar tractor and its driver could be spared from grading around the new red buildings, they started on their slow, lumbering way along the shoulder of the road up to where I had gone off. Fred came up in his own car with me and three of his men.

After some study they decided on the best route for drawing my car out; they got the tractor into position out ahead, and the tow chain all hooked up.

Just as I was about to get into my cab to steer, and as the men stood and glanced about once more before starting out, one of them said to Fred, "How the hell did he ever get in here anyhow? I'll bet he was drunk."

Fred glanced my way, then turned to the other and said in a lowered voice, though I caught the words, "He says not, but you can draw your own conclusions."

Glimpses of Perfectionism

THE LATE EVERETT WARNER, who was a well-known painter and for eighteen years Professor of Art at Carnegie Tech in Pittsburgh, had a summer home in Westmoreland, New Hampshire.

He was a most meticulous man. According to a fellow artist and neighbor of his, he was an extreme and comprehensive perfectionist in everything he did, including his carefully executed paintings. He could be quite exasperating to ordinary humans at times, perhaps a bit difficult at home, as I was later to conclude. And yet, rising above all such tendencies of character, he had been, as I was assured long afterward, the object of universal and sincere respect and affection, an active, concerned, cultured, and central figure once typical of the best of our "summer colonies."

Unfortunately, many of those extremes of character mentioned first were to show up during his close attention to a survey he asked me to make! He first wrote me two letters about it, both of them long and carefully worded, one being illustrated in great detail by a drawing in ink, pencil, and colored crayon. It all had to do with his concern—evidently mounting in previous weeks—about two old stone walls along the boundaries of his property which met to form his southwest corner.

During his own long study of old maps and deed records, some going back a century or more, Mr. Warner had discovered what most people would have regarded as entirely insignificant but perfectly understandable minor differences in compass bearings given for the two walls. His several sources of information indicated slight variations in the interior angle of the property lines formed by the walls meeting at the corner, the range being from about 118 degrees to about 121 degrees, as I recall it.

85

Whatever the true relationship between these walls was, as well as the absolute truth about a few other worrisome boundary matters, Mr. Warner was anxious to determine, accurately, once and for all.

It should be said that in New England the duties of a surveyor of rural lands include not only the definition of boundaries with appropriate care, but also the explanation and discussion of numerous problems, among them: local customs; traditions in the region; and the work, objectives and desired results of surveying. The whole purpose is not only to meet fully the tangible needs of a client but also to convey to him an understanding of the work so that he may see for himself that the right things have been adequately done.

Over thirty years ago I was far less alert to these intangible considerations than I hope I am now. Then too, Mr. Warner's wishes and anxieties, as well as his misconceptions of rural boundary lines, were all unusual to a degree entirely unpredictable to most anyone meeting him then for the first time. And so, on one hot August afternoon, with human frailty about evenly divided between us, the outlook was not propitious.

As my helper and I began taking successive courses paralleling the walls—by strictly conventional methods—I soon saw that our skeptical client was preparing to keep a separate set of notes of his own. As we proceeded he would constantly ask "What was that compass reading? . . . What was that distance again?". Soon he began to question the minor, seeming discrepancies in bearings, and I found myself not only trying to explain them but my methods as well. It all became very disturbing to us, both. It was a situation where most any technician might be subconsciously influenced to slant the readings of his instrument so as to minimize seeming inconsistencies, just to satisfy or impress someone or to avoid arguments —a tendency sure to lead away from technical fidelity—like a politician learning the uses of expedient rationalization.

Of course I began fervently to hope that our final result would fall within the range of past recorded figures. But alas, when we had traversed the first wall to its intersection with the second and then traversed that second wall to its end and then had sat down on the soft pasture grass and figured it out, we were a degree or so outside that range!

Although Mr. Warner had indicated other work he had wished done, this totally unsatisfactory outcome was so upsetting to him that, in a tired voice, he said, "I see no use in undertaking anything else."

In silence we all walked back toward the house; nothing more was said about surveying—then or ever.

In the yard, Mrs. Warner and their two sons were just returning in the car from swimming. The older boy came over to us and said, in a sincerely affectionate tone, "Well Dad, did you get your surveying done?"

Softly his father said, "All we need to do."

"That's good, Dad," the boy said.

When I asked for drinks of water before starting home, we were invited into the cool sitting room. Just then, Mrs. Warner, having now changed into a dark blue dress, came down the stairs, headed for the kitchen, but then turned sharply toward Mr. Warner and said, "Is that job done?"

"Yes", he said.

"Thank God!"

Landmark of a Hero

The Reverend John Williams, 1664-1728

MY BUSINESS TRAVELS over the past forty years have occasioned the constant use of various roads—now thoroughly familiar—along which are numerous landmarks, each memorable to me for some special reason. One might recall the scene of a highway accident for which I had made and displayed a map in court; or another farm surveyed for a client long remembered for being especially charming or detestable; still others were places made notable by history.

The most memorable of such landmarks, for me, is a modest monument placed in the fork of the roads at the junction of U.S. Route 5 and State Route 103, four miles north of Bellows Falls, Vermont, in the Township of Rockingham. Events relevant to it are as follows:

In February, 1704, Major Hertel de Rouville, of the French army in Canada, set out, with two-hundred French soldiers and 142 Maqua Indian tribesmen, for the purpose of attacking Deerfield, then one of the most prosperous but exposed of the English colonial outposts. The aim of the expedition was two-fold: to retard the growth of the English settlements, and to capture people that the colonial officials would ransom back, the average ransom being 200 pounds apiece.

The party came south, from the St. Lawrence Valley up the Richelieu River, up Lake Champlain, up the Winooski River, over the Green Mountain divide, down the White River, and down the Connecticut on the ice, reaching the north meadows of Deerfield on the evening of February 29th.

All that day a blizzard had blown, drifting and consolidating the snow to the very top of the great stockade on its northwest side. The attack was made some time after midnight, the savage

88

warriors easily scrambling up the drift, leaping over and down into the enclosure.

Once inside, they began breaking into the houses. They terrorized, fought, smashed, pillaged, burned, killed, and captured without letup till daybreak, by which time all buildings except the meetinghouse and one dwelling were reduced to smoldering ruins. Fifty-three people, including the negro servant and two youngest children of John Williams, the pastor, had met death. One hundred eleven were taken prisoners; 137 escaped, and of these only one or two undertook to carry the news to the next settlement to the south.

The journey north (its ultimate destination was Quebec City, 400 miles away) started at once and was relentlessly pushed ahead for four days and three nights, with little if any delay for fear of rescue parties. The pace was so great, the footing so exhausting, the condition and raiment of the colonists so inadequate, that about seventeen of them failed to keep up. Despite the prospect of a rich ransom for each prisoner and the diminishing chances of the expedition's being overtaken, the seventeen stragglers were callously killed by their guards simply to gain time. Mrs. Williams was among them, having fainted and fallen in an icy brook.

By the evening of Saturday, the 4th of March, they had reached a large flat area on the north bank of a tributary entering the Connecticut from the west. Observing the fatigue of captives and captors alike, the Reverend Williams urged de Rouville to allow a halt at this place. The latter, by then feeling secure from pursuit and reprisal and, no doubt, seeing the advantages of the place as a campground, agreed to a respite.

Ever since the attack, the "flock" of Mr. Williams had been separated—scattered out over a two- to four-mile stretch of the line of march. At the encampment, he had his first possible opportunity to bring them together. With his heroic devotion to them and to the duties of his office to God, and while sharing in full measure the common disaster and grief, he made the most of the situation. On the 5th, the Sabbath day, he assembled his people in a forest glade. While surrounded and guarded by a ring of Indians and French, and taking his text from Lamentations 1:18, he gave the first Protestant sermon and led the singing of the first Christian hymns ever heard in the wilderness later to become the State of Vermont.

The journey was resumed the following day. From then on everything went better. Many were given snowshoes; the pace was slackened with time taken out for hunting and fishing. Very few perished on the remainder of the journey to Canada.

At the end of two or three years, all captives had been ransomed back by Governor Dudley of the Massachusetts Bay Colony, with one noted exception: Eunice, a daughter of John Williams, who, according to Deerfield history, chose to remain in Canada and "married a savage and became one."

Two weeks after reaching Boston, Mr. Williams preached a sermon about the religious and other hardships he and his people had undergone during their captivity among Catholic Canadians, about which he later wrote a book, entitled *The Redeemed Captive Returned to Zion,* published in 1707.

John Williams was born in Roxbury, Massachusetts, in 1664. He was graduated from Harvard College in 1683, and was called to Deerfield in 1686. He was trained in the Calvinistic ideas of a jealous but righteous God. Though he suffered the tragedy of Deerfield as much as anyone, he regarded the event as a just punishment, and grimly did what he saw as his greatest duty, as he was to do throughout life, taking "the call" seriously.

After a short rest in Boston, he immediately journeyed out to Deerfield, helped rebuild the village, and lived and worked in peace the remaining twenty-two years of his life, passing away in 1728.

I am not the only one who has been moved by the meaning and inspiration of the life and character of this great man. That tributary of the Connecticut beside which the historic encampment and Christian gathering took place was named the Williams River in his honor, and in 1912 the Daughters of the American Revolution placed the monument in memory of those events of 1704. In 1931, Stephen Belaski painted a beautiful mural in the lobby of the then Bellows Falls High School, showing the captives gathered about their pastor as he reads from the open Bible, all of them surrounded by a ring of savages and French soldiers.

This story of Mr. Williams has held a growing fascination for me. The tragedy was a harder trial than most humans have ever been forced to bear, yet with iron will and devotion, Williams rallied all his faculties to meet the sudden demands of that pastoral "call." Though we may not espouse some of his beliefs, we have to admire the steadfast faith with which he held to his God—accepting His Judgment as justifiable and not to be questioned—and the inner and outer strength, the unselfishness, and the practical sense he showed in meeting the requirements of his office. Each time I pass his monument, no matter what the state of my own worries or what the problems of the world may be at the time, I breathe to him some little personal message of devotion for his almost-unparalleled example of faith and fortitude. He is one of my greatest heros.

The poem that follows was written to commemorate the 250th anniversary of the Deerfield captives assembled at Rockingham on March 5, 1704. I dedicated it to Stephen Belaski in appreciation of his painting of the event.

RECALLED AT THE WILLIAMS MONUMENT

Where the main routes called Five and One-O-Three
Part company to go their separate ways
To north and to northwesterly,
There stands a slant-topped granite stone
Set to preserve the memory that this
Is an historic, hallowed spot.
Upon this stone a tablet says that here,
Two and one-half centuries ago
In this dark, dread, and trackless land,
There stood the very earliest gathering
Of worshippers of the white man's God.

Caught in the new-world echoes
Of the wars between old empires,
They were the victims of a strange alliance
Of the French and Maqua tribes
Bent on rewards of ransom gold.
In an outpost of the old Bay colony
Their homes lay far behind, in ruins,
Within the desolate stockade

91

Mounted by a screeching savage horde
Upon the drifted snow one fiery, bloody dawn.

In the ensuing days of long, forced march
That brought them here they strove to keep
The grueling pace their captors set,
Made desperate by the penalty
Of death for those that caused delay.
Solace from loved-ones there was none;
Each struggled on, in spirit on his own,
Alone but for the revolting vigilance
And roving, speculative eye
Of his savage, jealous guard.

This was the trial to which their pastor's life
Of two score years led up, and found in him,
In his own words, "Sufficient grace
For what God should call us to."
And he has written, "I had a sense
Of divine rebukes which the holy God
Has seen meet, in spotless sovereignty,
To dispense to me, my family, and people."

Although, in outward mien, he stood aloof
To savage taunts and temporal power of those
That led him to a strange and distant land,
Yet he accepted them as instruments
Of Judgment, bitter but immutable,
Of a just God displaying indignation
At a professing people unreformed.

On the first Sabbath day he intervened
For rest, and "for revival in our bondage."
For the first time since their captivity
His people gathered to each other and to him.
Though held in awe and reverence
He now was closer drawn to them
By common ties of suffering,
All so equally weighed down by grief.

92

Under the open sky upon the trampled snow
Some stood and others knelt, but all
In various ways sent up their thanks
For this measure of a tentative deliverance.

He stood before them with uncovered head,
Gripping the open book of Holy writ,
And read, "The Lord is righteous,
For I have rebelled against his commands."
He prayed that mercy temper Judgment;
Counseled the will to bear repentantly
Afflictions of the Lord yet to be glorified,
And reformation here in life in preparation
For an holy boldness in the day of death.
And the accustomed silence of the forest,
For the first time in the land,
Broke with the songs of Zion's praise.

Upon the following break of day
He, with his people, rose, prepared,
And with a tread renewed, set forth.
Then with a stirring efficacy there came
Into his heart the words of psalms
For the strengthening of his faith and hope:
"I shall not die, but I shall live,
And declare the works of the Lord!"
But when they all had disappeared
Up the long river's wilderness trail,
Of him there yet remained, to live today,
Within this small and tributary valley,
And forever, his name and sacred memory.

A Deflated Vermonter

FLOYD JAQUITH of Weston had been in the lumber and woodlot business most of his life. He could drive teams, repair equipment, fell trees, scale and load logs, and grade lumber. But he also had a keen eye for some of the more intangible factors as well: estimation of timber, values and prices, human nature, and the psychology of horses. He loved to tell story after story of his long career in this field of rural endeavor with its pitfalls, sharp dickering, and exciting business hazards and possibilities. Take it all around, you would have felt no need to worry for him; he obviously could take care of himself among the best of them.

In 1945 he sold three adjoining tracts of land in the adjacent town of Landgrove to Mr. J. Edgar Rhoads, a venerable and meticulous Quaker gentleman from Delaware, for a summer place.

The easternmost of these three tracts comprised eighty acres, and there was a very fine stand of excellent pine timber in the south part which Floyd did not wish to sell. So during the negotiations it was agreed that he might reserve all the timber lying south of a line which would be run across the lot from the west side to the east side. The purchaser agreed to pay for the survey of all three tracts, as well as for the running and marking of the reservation line. Sitting in the office of the purchaser's attorney as the parties to the entire transaction were ironing out all the details, Floyd tried to visualize the situation down in those woods. What definite point could be designated in the deed and later shown as the point for a surveyor to begin when running the reservation line? Floyd, the only one in the room who really knew all the various landmarks in the area felt under some pressure to make a decision; quite likely there lurked in the back of his

94

mind the advisability of holding up negotiations another day or so while he actually went down to take a final look. In the end he took a chance on his memory, and said he thought the northeast corner of the Cody farm would be agreeable to him, and accordingly this was typed into the deed, which was then signed by him and duly witnessed.

Mr. Rhoads' attorney engaged me to do the surveying, saying that Mr. Jaquith would go with me and show and explain everything.

A day was set to begin: January 28, 1946. The preceding afternoon, my helper, Gordon Cunningham, and I drove to Weston and found and put up at the Weston Inn. Incidentally, this was the beginning of our many years of family and business patronage. The Inn, after some years of idleness, had just been refurbished and opened for business by Miss Nancy Baird, a young woman of great charm and capability, taste and culture, poise and wit.

The following day was to prove in every way a bad one for Floyd from beginning to end. It dawned cold and overcast, as it was to remain all day. Floyd walked down to the center of town, there to wait for us with growing annoyance, from seven o'clock until eight-thirty, leaning on the cold iron railing surrounding the "village green," then white with a foot of snow. He could, of course, just as well have stepped over to the Inn and sat by the fire.

"Where the hell you fellows been all this time?" Floyd asked as he got into my car. On my explaining that Miss Baird did not serve breakfast till eight o'clock, he said, "Well, you tell Miss Baird she would never get anywhere in the lumber business if she can't get breakfast before eight o'clock in the morning." (Being told this, that evening, she said, "You tell Mr. Jaquith I don't care if I never get anywhere in the lumber business.")

Over the hills and snowy roads, that dark and forbidding day, we drove to Landgrove where our work was to be.

After showing us the tracts near the road, which we could survey later without his guidance, he led us down through the brushy pastures to the west line of the east lot and then down along that to the Cody corner, at an old hemlock tree with blazes and old fence-wire grown deep into the wood.

From this point, surveying easterly, we had gone but a short way when Floyd saw, to his sudden consternation, that he had made a great and grievous mistake of judgment. As we proceeded across the lot, and he saw how much valuable timber stood to our left, north of our line, his dismay mounted. I was to realize later how he was now beginning to imagine that he had, on the day of "the closing," allowed himself to be cajoled into unwise and ill-considered haste in suggesting a location for the reservation line. Following us, his constant glances to the north were accompanied by cries of anguish, self-condemnation and doubt: "How can this be? What have I done?" And his eyes rolled upward and his hands made gestures of entreaty for mercy from Heaven. No doubt at some point he began to contemplate an inevitable confrontation with his partner—an added burden on his soul.

As Gordon and I finished out the day, we were trailed by a once proud but now deflated lumberman plagued by the chagrin of material loss and—just as bad, if not worse—a vanished prestige and self-respect.

Driving back again over the hills and snowy roads, mostly in silence as each of us nursed his own special thoughts, we reached the village at dusk—cold, tired, and hungry. For Gordon and me there loomed ahead, in our minds' eyes, the vision, very soon to be realized, of hot coffee and cheering entertainment in front of a blazing fire to be followed by good food, bright conversation with our fascinating hostess, and thoughts of a profitable day's work accomplished. But for Floyd! Only mortification.

Standing by the car for a moment as we separated for the night, and while shaking his head as if exhausted by the thought, he said, "I don't know which is worst, to lose all that timber or to have my neighbors know I was beat by a city man."

On Barnett Hill

WHILE SURVEYING over the rocky, ridged hills on which lay a large tract of pasture, woodlands, and mowing then constituting a country estate just purchased by a new owner, I gradually learned, from my helper, Henry Mercer, a local farm neighbor, his version of the story of "Old Man Barnett"—his designation of the legendary man who had named the hill.

According to Henry, the "old man" had been a rich merchant down in the city; he had come up many years ago and "built him a summer home out of thousands and thousands of feet of lumber and hundreds of boatloads of stun." Looking at the huge, part formal, part rustic mansion, you could see how eminently correct Henry's description was.

Mr. Barnett had been very well liked by the local people, and enjoyed with them a long, friendly, and mutual respect. With Mrs. Barnett, it had been different; local neighbors simply never could get to know her. She was "always tearing around considerable," during the "season" when they would be up, always in "very important circles"—circles in which, according to Henry, "the old man could never keep up."

During his last years, Mr. Barnett had been ailing and despondent much of the time. One evening, although he had been unusually sick and was confined to his bed in their city home, his wife just *"had* to go to a *very important* dinner party," so Henry said, with sneering scorn. Some bitter sense of hopelessness or neglect must have overcome old Mr. Barnett, for he was found later that night, having ended his own life.

Henry spoke of young Barnett, the son, who had come up to the place only occasionally and had eventually sold it to "this bird" (the new owner we were then working for).

I asked more about the son, and what sort of man he had been. "Well," Henry said, "he wa'n't much; he wa'n't no such man as his father was . . . just puttered around, fur as I could see . . . I'll tell you, he done one thing I didn't think much of; he took that razor 't his father cut his throat with and sold it to me for a quarter; that's what I call pretty damn small!"

I could not help asking him—recalling there is never a sale without a purchase—what he would have done with it, if in that young man's place. With great dignity and vehemence, he said, "I would have destroyed it!"

After a few more stretches of the tape, as we pursued the job, I said, "Henry, if you still have that razor, what do you do with it?"

"I shave with it," he said.

The Man at the Crossing

THE MOST COLORFUL PERSONALITY in railroading around here, during the years of our patronage, was Francis Hogan, the guard at the crossing at Bellows Falls, Vermont. This is where we usually met trains.

Francis was a one-man institution. When trains of the Connecticut River Line of the Boston and Maine came through, his job was to stand at the center of Depot Street and hold up a hand sign that said STOP. The crossing was next to the passenger station and baggage office, and Francis made the most of the situation as a social outlet for his restless, outgoing spirits.

When he wasn't holding up the sign, he strode around the platforms and the street greeting and waving at everyone, known or unknown, whose eye he could catch; and with his high, penetrating voice and cheerful tone, he dominated the scene as much as one man could. His presence greatly accentuated the usual stir so natural to the comings and goings at "train time," his relationship to the whole being like that of the crashing cymbals in an orchestra. His part was not the calm, restrained and personalized attentiveness, the polished urbanity, of the legendary Asa Porter, beloved conductor of the "Boat Train" from Boston to Fall River, who was as the melodious cello of that far away, more sophisticated setting. Rather, it was a simple, bombastic gregariousness and good-will constantly overflowing the shallow cup of his intermittent, certainly not taxing, duty.

The routine monotony of his job, practically a one-motion act geared to a train schedule, allowed a man of his nature to bring a touch of joviality to the traditional pageantry which accompanied the crowds of dressed-up travelers and their loved-ones milling about a passenger train.

Such pageantry is now a passing memory, but certainly one that is dear to the hearts of all whose travels brought them to railroad stations like this one—if indeed any other like this could be!—with its self-appointed greeter seeming to endow the mere physical facilities of a railroad with a living, present, human soul.

The agreeable remarks Francis would make were always appropriate to the conditions of the moment, or the season.

In the spring, there would be the roar and rumble of flood waters—always of great public interest and concern—as the great river poured over the dam and dashed upon the rocks below, throwing up clouds of spray to envelope the bridge, just north of the station.

In summer, the intense rays of the sun and its reflected heat from asphalt or planks would drive everyone to the cool shade under the platform roofs.

In the fall, there was the fog, the chill, and the drizzling rain enshrouding the whole river valley in general—and this depot in particular—with an air of gloom and a prophecy of the rigors of the season just ahead.

And in winter, the driving snow and icy blasts would often keep us confined in the station, maybe late at night, especially at Christmas time when all manner of delays caused a near-complete abandonment of the schedules. Delayed hours of arrival, chalked up on the bulletin board, were constantly revised to yet later hours. Once, as I went outside in the cold again for the forty-leventh time to listen for some hopeful sound from down river, a man asked: "How late is the New York train?" I told him, "Forty-five minutes, so far." Cheerfully he said, "Oh, well, that's par for the course." (As a young fellow, I used to wonder what the Hamilton people meant by advertising "The Watch of Railroad Accuracy.")

The monotony of some of those long waits, was sure to be mitigated by the pointed remarks of the crossingman, himself restless with the delay.

As well as performing his regular job, holding up the Stop sign, Francis would gladly answer your questions, share your

100

frustrations, explain the delays and recount railroad lore. He would also make you feel you were a most welcome guest of the Company whose loyal and voluble spokesman he had become.

Early one bitter morning, a southbound train stood across Depot Street halting traffic a few minutes, leaving Francis free to mingle with those on the platform, vigorously swinging his arms about him to keep warm. A little old man, whose belongings were tied to a stick and slung over his shoulder in traditional immigrant fashion, asked in a feeble voice if this was the train to Brattleboro. "Yes, sir," said Francis who then gave him the whole works: "Westminister, Putney, Brattleboro, Greenfield, Springfield, Hartford, New Haven, Ne' York"—by the end of this sequence, his roving glances having long since strayed to some entirely different quarter.

When my wife took eight of her nursery school children to watch the trains, Francis immediately assumed the roll of host and told them all about the railroad. Then he added a touch typical of his eager and generous nature: he invited them all into his little "crossingman's hut"; its small size and the warm feeling of the little pot-bellied stove on that chilly day entranced the children. And when he took down his dinner basket from a high shelf, lifted out a cake and cut each child a piece, his success was complete!

There were other occasions when we used to see our girls off to school or college or a foreign land, and after seeing them into the cars with a few last loving words, we would stand about the platform to wave a final goodbye. Francis, picturing our thoughts, would praise the advantages of education which life had denied him, and he would recite his very correct imaginings of our joys and hopes and longings for them as they left for the long months in far-away places.

On one of these departures, he said to me, "Well, Mr. Chase, I know just how you feel. But it won't be too long. You're standing here with me today. But in a few months you'll be back here again. You'll be waiting way down there at the end of the walk—I seen you down there before! You'll hear that whistle, and pretty soon you'll see that headlight comin' through the tunnel. And she'll be back! Ah! That'll be the day!" Soon there was heard the old call: "Board!" "Goodbye, Mr. Chase, and good luck to your daughter." Francis then took his place in the street, and held up the sign to stop traffic. (By this time, passengers on this line were carried in connected pairs of "diesel-ized" Buddliner cars, which when southbound and making the stop at Bellows Falls, were halted beside the station and just even with the north edge of Depot Street.) Diesel engines began to rev up and take hold; there was a gentle blast of the air-horn and the car growled and ground its way across the street, gained speed as it passed the south platform, rumbled over the steel bridge across the canal, passed through the tunnel under the village square, the rear end of the car visible for only a moment after emerging at the far end into the bright morning sunlight before rounding a curve and disappearing—leaving a sudden pang of emptiness and some slight sense of eternity.

But a few words of simple reassurance and friendship remained.

Alas, however, the routine character of the guard's job at the crossing was its downfall; automatic electric signals took over in 1959. No change around here in recent years better epitomizes the de-humanizing of life by materialistic science than this replacement of a living man by inanimate steel posts with their blinking, garish red eyes, their cold hearts of solenoidal switches, their nerves of copper wire, and their voices of clanging brass

102

—that will never answer a question or pay the slightest attention to you or me.

For us, when Francis left the crossing and the depot, most of the sense of "community of interest" that there had been in our relations with the railroad went with him.

If the skeletonization and timing of schedules and the deterioration of service had been part of a deliberate plan of the Company's to drive passenger traffic away, the general aspect and atmosphere of the whole facility would have been about what it became. But I feel sure that Francis Hogan, had he been serving to the end, would have done so helpfully and cheerfully, and, like Asa Porter, would have been no part or victim of the sagging morale and declining *esprit de corps* that accompanied the demise of this once-great institution of travel.

A Confused Witness

THE TRIAL AT BRATTLEBORO was dragging along into the second week. As a few narrow beams of the hot July afternoon sun stole around edges of the drawn shades, the natural antagonism of the contending parties seemed greatly mitigated by the common effort, in which all in the courtroom joined, to resist the heat, keep awake and upright. This was not made any easier by the monotonous reading of deeds and other documents and entering them as evidence, and all the other dull routine of a case based on record title.

But the trial did have its moments.

The attorney for the plaintiffs called to the stand, as his next witness, an old friend of the family—a plump, vigorous, gray-haired little lady of sixty-five, decked out in a light blue dress and a cool, wide-brimmed hat. The very way she took the stand and answered the clerk's mumbling of the oath at once charged the atmosphere with a state of alert expectation.

From the attorney's very first question she was a great help. Why, yes, from childhood she could remember, as if it were yesterday, that south line of the old farm she used to come to, summers. Yes, indeed, it was right along a row of old marked beech trees. What sort of marks were they? Axe marks, of course! Must have been made by a surveyor, cut deep into the wood.

The attorney's air of triumph indicated his satisfaction in at last showing the court that he and his clients had tangible evidence on the long lost and disputed boundary line. He pressed his advantage with just one more question: "How high were these marks?"

"How high?" said she, very happy to oblige (and, it is barely possible, a bit rattled as to the matters of timing, and under a misconception as to the manner of the growth of trees), "Why, some were three feet high, some six feet, some twelve."

Dead silence fell upon the scene. Amused, incredulous glances began darting from one to another, then turned toward the judge who was now leaning forward, to ask: could he have heard her correctly that some of these marks were twelve feet high?

"Yes, you did," she said, with a grim and determined defensiveness.

"Do you realize that would be about the height of this room?" She merely glanced up the wall, but said nothing.

The attorney, clearing his throat, approached the witness in an effort to get matters back under control, and, with great caution put forth a few gentle suggestions—in the form of questions, of course—calculated to get some modification of her testimony. If she had been as bright, quick, and charming as some women are in such a spot, the whole thing might have been laughed off as a momentary slip of the tongue, and the reasonable parts of her testimony would have continued to stand firm for whatever they were worth. But, alas, for him, no saving measure of reconsideration would she give him. Sticking stubbornly to her guns, she would retract nothing.

The attorney simply could not hide his loss as to how to proceed; for him, as for everyone else, a breathing spell was in order, and the judge declared a recess. With an immediate scraping of chairs and a low buzzing of voices, people rose and started for the hallways.

The defendant—humorous, philosophical, and stubborn—after seven years of study of his own case with my help as a surveyor, had long since become entirely relaxed in sitting back and letting the plaintiffs and their attorney do their utmost, confident that with enough time and rope they would "hang themselves." Now, as he rose from his chair, and walked into the hall, his pensive smile at the floor was a sign that something was brewing in his ever-active mind.

Toward the end of the recess, as I was standing with him at the end of the hall, and after a backward glance in the direction of "judge's chambers," he beckoned his two attorneys to him, and in a low voice said, "Boys, I've been thinking over what the old lady said about those axe marks. Come to think of it, that wasn't so funny as it might seem at first. Now, we know that in the old days, the snow used to get awfully, awfully deep in winter up in those hills—lots deeper than it does now. Then, too, men used to be bigger, and stronger, and taller than they are today. No doubt, they had longer-handled axes than we do now. Well, added to all that, maybe just a little prevarication could make up the difference!"

Our Needs Not Always Known

I HAVE OFTEN TRIED to anticipate the course of events which may eventually lead me to places long contemplated. And driving along a main valley road on frequent surveying trips, I used to wonder about an unusually large and fine set of farm buildings visible far up on a pastured hillside and whether destiny would ever lead me there.

Finally it did. Word came, through a hired man, that the owner wished to see me about surveying his farm. So I went up. A maid met me at the door of the large farm house, and I was ushered into a small room furnished more or less as an office, and told that Mr. Trobelski would see me soon.

Seated on the north side of a large table and gazing out a west window over a beautiful field bordered by sugar-lot maples, all golden in the afternoon sun, I wondered what the results of the visit might be. Some such engagements have proven of surprising and memorable outcome.

Presently Mr. Trobelski came in, shook hands courteously and thanked me for coming and then took a chair opposite me, his actions all in the manner of a man pursued by chronic ill health and fatigue. His skin was pale, his body overweight, his whole attitude somber. All his words and few gestures were those of a tired man, prematurely aging—though perhaps he was only sixty.

Mr. Trobelski said his farm consisted of several large tracts, bought at various times, each estimated at so many acres, more or less, and described in deeds only in general terms and with some boundaries poorly shown or in question. He needed it surveyed, mapped, and accurately measured. He was most anxious to have me do his work.

He would have to know, he said, just what the work would cost.

This would be a difficulty. I undertook to explain how indefinite such work and all its requirements usually are, and why, therefore, costs based on time and expenses after the work is done are the only right basis for rendering a bill. This did not satisfy him, but seemed merely to add to the burdens of uncertainty already weighing on his soul.

Mr. Trobelski had been a successful businessman in eastern Europe in the 1930's, but with the spread of fear, uncertainty, and the prospects of war, social and economic upheavals and chaos, he had decided to seek refuge in the New World. Here also he had evidently felt himself in some measure a victim of economic injustice and sharp deals, this time in the traditional manner in which Americans have taken advantage of refugees from old-world tyranny, want, overcrowding and war—"The Uprooted", as Oscar Handlin so movingly describes them in his book of that title. This feeling would almost certainly have come to any immigrant of more than average means and who was attempting to establish himself by renovating an old New England farm. And so, in view of his hazardous life and his physical and spiritual condition, it is understandable that Mr. Trobelski felt he must guard against mistreatment while getting his property surveyed, and so refuse to have the work done till a price was agreed upon.

After stating again my reasons for not undertaking the work on that basis, I leaned forward and said, "Sir, you could easily be cheated even under a contract laying down all details, conditions, and objectives at a fixed charge, providing a surveyor were dishonest. The best assurance of overall satisfaction for you would be to take time and ask a number of people in your region what surveyors they would recommend; then talk with one or more of the surveyors, select one of them yourself, and put him to work. Keep in touch with him as to his feelings and progress, and *trust* him. That is the best you can do."

"I have already inquired," he said, "and everyone favors you."

"Then why can you not trust me?" I asked. He simply insisted again that he must know the cost in advance.

When I said, for the third time, that I could not do business that way, he said, with evident sorrow, "Well, I am deeply disappointed . . . This work is very urgent and important to me."

I felt a growing compassion for this man. But why, I wondered—with all the pressing things that always needed doing on a large farm—was this survey of his boundaries so important to him now, after some years of peaceful occupancy. It all seemed to me an unreasonable and over-riding obsession with him.

We continued to talk; as we did so, there came to mind a dim memory from my childhood. I recalled a story from the *Tales* of Tolstoy, read to us by my mother at least fifty years before. The part of the story most relevent to this visit with the troubled Mr. Trobelski was, to the best of my memory, as follows:

An old shoemaker, in a small village in Russia, one winter's day found a naked young man huddled and shivering on the doorstep of the church. With instant compassion, he put his own coat about the young man, brought him home, warmed him, clothed him, fed him, and gave him a bed. In the weeks and months following, he gave him a home, trained him, and took him on as an apprentice. In time the young man so mastered the trade of shoemaker as to be worthy of faith and trust and gained respected wisdom and judgment.

The young man said little. The only explanation he was ever to give of his presence on the church step that cold day was that, as an angel and servant of God in Heaven, he had—because of his lack of faith—been banished to Earth until he should learn a needed lesson: What Men Live By—The Power of Love.

One day a rich and arrogant nobleman came in a sleigh, strode into the shop, followed by his driver who was carrying a bundle of very choice leather, and demanded to know if, from these goods they could fashion him some certain kind of winter boots. If they could, well and good; if not, say so now, but if they took this rare leather and spoiled it, he would bring down his wrath upon them. The old shoemaker turned to his apprentice and said, "Shall we take the work?" The answer was yes.

Then the nobleman left with his driver, climbed into the sleigh, drew up the robes, and drove away. The apprentice retired with the goods to his bench, and soon began to measure and cut.

Some days later the old shoemaker came over to see how the younger man's work was progressing, and observed that he was just finishing up a pair of shoes. But then, suddenly and to his utter horror, he saw that they were not at all the sort of boots ordered by their haughty customer, and in his rising anguish he cried out, "Why, my boy! You have used up that precious leather on the kind of shoes used for burying the dead! What is the meaning of this? You heard what the nobleman said. This will ruin us!"

Just then there came a knock at the door; the driver of the great nobleman's sleigh came in, and said, "Good people, my master has died, and his lady has asked me to say that if you have not already used up the leather, will you please make a pair of burial shoes for her husband."

Thereupon the young shoemaker took his finished work, dusted it off, wrapped it up and handed it to the driver who then paid them, thanked them courteously, bid them a kind Good Day and went out, climbed into the sleigh, drew up the robes and drove away.

When the old shoemaker got his mind oriented to all that had just taken place, he said to the other, "How did you happen to do what you did?"

"When the nobleman was here, ordering the winter boots," the young man said, "I saw, standing for a moment behind him, an old friend of mine, The Angel of Death, and he made a sign to me indicating that this great man, contrary to his belief, would not need any more winter boots, but would soon need shoes suitable for burial."

This much of the story, as well as I have been able to recall it, lay dormant in the back of my mind since childhood, but suddenly came to the fore as I sat contemplating all I could see of this would-be patron of my profession, a man so sure he knew what he needed most, yet who seemed actually to be in far more urgent need of spiritual and physical renewal. From thus gazing absentmindedly at him as the story emerged, I looked over and beyond the bowed head of the dejected Mr. Trobelski, and for just an instant there stood before my mind's eye a faint, fleeting, and ghostly outline of that Angel of Death seen by the cobbler's young apprentice.

Then suddenly aware again of my actual surroundings, I pulled myself together, not ever wishing to entertain baseless or morbid thoughts. I returned resolutely to reality and said, "Sir, I suggest that you take time to think over what I have told you. Let me know when I may call on you again, for I am sure we can get together somehow."

But evidently Fate had already ordained it otherwise: all his burdensome concerns—about neighbors and loved ones; about land surveyors, boundaries, and acreages; his health and all other material and worldly prospects—were to be lifted from his beleaguered spirit one month later, and forever.

Land Enough

ONE SUMMER DAY as we sat in the woods resting and eating lunch during the survey of a woodlot line for Seth Holden, just for something to say, I asked Seth if he owned very much land around there. This was his answer:

Do I own much land around here? Good God yas, too much! Why, I got sixty, seventy acres right here side o' this line you're on now. Out to the west o' here I got a lot more, I forgit which town it's in, don't know 's I give a damn. . . . while back I come damn near gittin' 'bout 200 more 't ol' man Williston used to own. . . . You see when I was young I used to live with Herb Williston and his ol' woman. Herb was a hell of nice ol' man, now I tell ye, but her? Good God, she was a damned old bitch. . . . why, couldn't nobody get along with her. . . . she's just the same now, too. . . . Well, Herb had this lot I'm tellin' ye bout, had some almighty nice timber on it, one of the best growin' stands I ever see.

One day, him and me and Hen Stafford was down on that lot, and I looked around at them big trees and I says, kind o' half to myself and half to Herb, I says, "By God, I wished I had a lot like this." Well, you know what he done? He looked right at me, and he says, "By God, I'll see't you git it!" Course, I never thought nothin' bout what he said then. But bout a year after that I happened to hear he'd wrote another will, and t'want but a short time after that that he kicked off and they took him for his last ride, right out to the bone yard.

Next day Hen Stafford come to me and says, "Seth," he says, "did you know that just before Herb died he'd wrote another will? Well, they say't he did. Well, do you remember that time when me and you and him was down on his big pine lot and you

112

says to him how you wished you had a lot like that and he says he'd see 't you got it? You remember that? I been thinkin' bout that ever since that time and I come to think he might o' meant it. You ought to know," Hen says to me, "Herb Williston thought a hell of a lot more o' you than he ever did o' that old woman o' his!"

Then I commenced to think about it, and I says to myself, I says, "By God, 'twont do no harm to go down try to find out what the new will says." So I went down. That damned old woman must o' seen me through the window just's I was comin' round back to the kitchen door, and she must o' knowed what I wanted, cause just's I got where I could see through the door int' the room, she grabbed up some kind of paper off the kitchen table; she give me an almighty savage look, an' fore I could open my trap to speak, by the Jesus Christ, she raised up the teakittle and shoved that paper right int' the God damn stove. . . . So I never did git that lot o' Herb's. . . . But, have I got land enough? Good God, yas, too much.'

High Compliment
or The Salesman Foiled

ONE DAY a young salesman of kitchen stoves called on us. He looked over the twenty dollar secondhand old black cast iron, cabinet Glenwood kitchen range which had served us so well for the fifteen years since we had first set up housekeeping here. He also showed us the very neat, salesman's scale model of the product he sold.

We were not then at all interested in making a change, but since we were much attracted to him and as it was about noon, we invited him to stay to lunch.

During the ensuing visit we talked of many things, returning at frequent intervals, of course, to the matter of stoves.

When the meal was over, he thanked us for it and for the visit, but added: "All this time you have had me stumped. One of the principles of salesmanship of household appliances is to first determine which—the husband or the wife—is the boss, and then concentrate on that one; in this case I simply cannot tell."

A Northerly Point of View

I WAS EMPLOYED to survey and make a map of a large tract of land in Vermont and to prepare to testify regarding it in court at Woodstock during the lawsuit of Ripchick and Osadnick vs. The International Paper Company. The defendant company had bought and cut off all the spruce timber on the tract, but there was an ambiguous boundary line, and the company was being sued for having extensively cut over into the adjoining land of the plaintiffs.

The lot was bounded on the north by an old road running east and west, this road being the only one by which the lot could be reached and the timber brought out. Otherwise, the lot was bounded mostly by old walls and delapidated pasture fence wire, and, then, of course, the lost or obliterated line now in question.

My map was of prime importance in this case. Together with whatever verbal testimony I might give, it was the only means by which the jury was to see an impartial and graphic representation of the lot and its boundaries presented by an "expert" witness (anyone bringing special, technical training to bear on a case). This was because the opposing attorneys had agreed to deny the jury a "view" of the premises. The attorneys for the plaintiffs feared that the men on the jury might see a row of old, blazed trees up to which the Company's woods foreman—with some justification—had thought it safe to cut. On the other hand, the attorneys for the defendant feared that the esthetic and conservationist sensibilities of the half-dozen women on the jury would be offended by the complete "slaughter" of all the trees on the desecrated hillsides, where only weed trees, stumps, and brush remained—a forbidding aspect indeed, a tangled mess left on the land by modern logging and big business.

I was asked to take the witness stand, duly sworn in, and then asked to present my map, which was then entered as a "plaintiff's exhibit" and tacked up on the board in full view of the courtroom. I was questioned and cross-questioned about the lot, the survey, and the map—until it was felt the entire situation was clear to everyone.

The next witness was John Sesoff. "Johnnie Seesaw", as he was called, was now a little old man, but purportedly he had a keen memory. Twenty or thirty years before he had cruised the entire lot in question, searching for the clearest, straightest and most uniform spruce trees to be used as beams in the construction of "Johnnie Seesaw's Bromley Mountain Ski Club", the well-known lodge on Route 11 in Peru.

When he was questioned by the attorney for the plaintiffs about the lot and its boundaries and the stand of timber those many years ago, Johnnie seemed to recall everything clearly. Then he was asked to look at the map and state whether, in his opinion, it was a fair representation of the lot. He studied it for some time in silence and finally answered that he could not understand it. So the attorney reviewed the details of the map for him, pointing to the cut-over area, the boundaries as far as known, including the old town road running along the north side and a lane leading southerly into the lot—over which the witness had just said he had drawn out the timber used for the lodge.

By this time everyone in the room was especially attentive, for this witness, now seeming to falter, should have been able to give some of the very most important testimony in the entire case.

Asked once more if he now could understand the map, he said he could not, for something was definitely wrong. But he continued to study the map; then he cocked his head first one way, then the other. Finally, as if with a sudden and new inspiration, he stood up, leaned way over on his hands and one knee so as to view the map from an inverted position. "Ah!" came his triumphant but slightly muffled voice, "Now I can understand!"

116

Getting up, he glanced all around the room, at last spotting me sitting in the front spectators' bench, and, pointing in ridicule, said, "That surveyor! He's all wrong. He's got that lot upside down!"

Judge Shangraw used the gavel to restore proper courtroom solemnity—but only after he had nearly attained it himself.

Knowing One's Neighbors

FRANCIS PALMER, a native and life-long resident of Grafton, Vermont, had for many years kept the one small grocery store in the center of the village. I believe he had been a "lister", which accounted in part for his being *the* man that anyone, especially a surveyor, would consult on the history and location of all the old farms and boundary lines. This was his hobby, and he had made a good start composing a map of the town with all its old properties shown.

Francis knew his neighbors very well, too.

I once had occasion to ask him where I might put up for the night. He said a Mrs. Daniels might give the use of a room, and he directed me up the street to her house.

She was an elderly lady, of aristocratic bearing, her grey hair becomingly controlled and embellished with a wide red ribbon, and she was the widow of a noted Chicago lawyer. Grafton had been their "second" home. She now stayed year round, living in genteel austerity; she took in "selected tourists", and was gradually having to liquidate her large collection of antiques. (A fine pair of brass candlesticks now on our mantel serve to remind me of the pleasant visit with her on this occasion.)

After some questions about my work, home, other acquaintances in Vermont and my immediate activities in Grafton that day, she showed me to my room. But when the question of dinner arose, she leaned wearily against a door jamb and with a dejected gaze at the floor, said in a high wavering, and plaintive voice, "I am sorry that I no longer have the strength to do cooking for guests this late in the day. But if you will go down to Francis Palmer's store, he will have something you can bring here, and you will be most welcome to use my stove and kitchen to prepare it yourself." I said I would be very glad to do that.

As I entered the store, Francis, with a slight, self-satisfied grin, said, "You're going to stay up to Mrs. Daniels' place, aint you?"

I named a few items I would like. He took these off the various shelves, one by one, and placed them on the counter. When he had done them up and I had paid for them, he then leaned, as with weary arms and back, over the counter. With a tired and dejected gaze down at the package, and in a high, wavering, and plaintive voice, said, "I spose she just didn't have the strength to cook your supper for yuh."

A Victim of World Affairs

In September 1955, I was employed by Mr. and Mrs. James Campbell Lewis to survey and mark a considerable portion of the boundary lines of their large property in Cornish, New Hampshire.

According to their deeds, one of the adjoining owners was Learned Hand. Surprising as it may seem, I could not "place him" at first, though I had heard the name in some connection or other.

Following my regular custom of going to meet adjoining owners, to inform them of my purpose in traversing property lines, and to seek their opinions and points of view, I called at the Hand house. Mrs. Hand greeted me graciously, and, on being informed of my purpose, said to go right ahead. Then I asked what her husband was noted for. She said, with an air of great respect, "Oh, he is a very famous judge!" After that I recalled that I had heard of a well-known judge of that name.

Later, during this work at Cornish I met Judge Hand, and we had a pleasant though brief visit, largely confined to the matter of the Lewis survey. (Naturally I now wish I had taken time to get to know him and his ideas much better. But "golden opportunities" are so often neglected—chances to broaden our vision and perspective on life—through obliviousness or ignorance.)

At the end of my first day's work, I had reason to conclude that two certain adjacent lines—one of 259 feet and one of sixty-three feet and differing in bearing by only fourteen degrees, which together comprised Judge Hand's south line—could better be replaced by one straight line, thus eliminating one corner in an exposed and vulnerable position which would be difficult to mark permanently and maintain.

That evening I presented this proposal to the Lewises. In doing so, I had to admit that this would mean a concession of about a twentieth of an acre—not located anywhere near their buildings and certainly a negligible fraction of their holdings of two-hundred acres or more—yet seeming to me a very practical change to make.

Up to this time I had had no reason to take particular note of the personalities of my clients. They had merely shown me their deeds that morning and asked me to follow their descriptions of lines and corners, now obliterated, obscure or otherwise uncertain.

My recollections of Mr. Lewis remain indistinct. But Mrs. Lewis will remain a vivid memory as long as I live. She was dark of complexion, fine of feature, and of somewhat less than average height, but this was more than compensated for by an authoritative bearing and commanding personality; she at once held my fascinated attention. Dark glasses, never removed, did for Mrs. Lewis what most wearers of such trappings of seeming affectation desire—but seldom achieve: never to reveal all that lies behind one's personal position, purpose or attitude. Her deadly seriousness was never relaxed. Incidentally, in an intense and passionate way she was one of the first "environmentalists" (as we would call them now) I had ever met; her special concern was the unknowable dangers to which we were subjecting the atmosphere surrounding the earth by electric power lines, poles, towers, telephones, and radios whose man-imposed electronic waves and fields of magnetic force endangered all forms of biological life on earth. I was not then, nor am I now, in any position to argue against her beliefs. But her thinking and strong feelings about society's overall acts upon our finite earth and its forces, resources, and natural processes—based apparently upon wide study and knowledge—commanded respect. Even her hair-do, jewelry, and flashy gown but added to her air of distinction —as did also her perfect English, even though with a European accent.

This may explain why Mr. Lewis made little or no impression on me that evening.

Needless to say, it was Mrs. Lewis who would instantly formulate and present the Lewis position in response to my suggestion.

"We will never agree to any such thing!" she cried—and with what seemed to me a bewilderingly sudden and inordinate intensity of feeling.

Whatever last words of meek defense I may have uttered were repulsed by her forceful ultimatum: "We will never concede anything to that man!"

After some thought, and with rising curiosity I ventured to say, "Mrs. Lewis, there is evidently some hard feeling here against Judge Hand. Would you care to tell me about it?"

"Yes I will! He freed Judy Coplon."

Only with some effort did I then vaguely recall that a woman by such a name—I thought it was Copeland—had been arrested for conveying U.S. government secrets, papers, or something, to the Russians but had been released later because of technical irregularities in the manner of her detection and apprehension; and Judge Hand came dimly to mind in connection with the case.

I wondered just why the Coplon affair should have put Mrs. Lewis in such a state of mind. So I asked my one last question.

She leaned forward and undertook—effectively!—in just three words to make clear once and for all her position in the world, and to end any further discussion of relations with the Judge; her words were uttered with unrestrained contempt and hate but imbued also with suppressed grief and deep personal injury: "*I am Hungarian!*" she said, and slumped back in her chair.

Certainly no three words have ever hit me so hard, silenced me so completely, or reduced me to speechless humility as did those of the spiritually-beleaguered Mrs. Lewis of Cornish, New Hampshire. Their result, ever afterward, was a deep sympathy and abiding respect. And what I felt for her then is augmented each time I consider dates and events, to realize how, only fourteen months later, she must have suffered great additional anguish and sorrow for friends, relatives, and country during the Hungarian uprising and its merciless suppression by the Russian Army in November 1956.

The experience pointed up to me the divisiveness, cruelty and far-reaching repercussions of war and tyranny—by nations and individuals—in our world society with its spiderweb-like interrelated sensitivity, creating in human affairs a sort of chronic chaos in which it must be difficult—even for good and wise men, let alone the common run—to choose correctly between greater and lesser evils and goods. I have, of course, in recent years, learned something of Judge Hand's reasons for what he did in the Coplon case. But still, no matter how right, just and wise our decisions may seem, it is obvious that in our complex world, some are not going to agree, some are going to suffer, often with bitterness.

That evening, at the Lewises, when I finally was able to get my mind back to my part in the situation, and as I rose to leave for the night, I simply said, "I will re-establish all lines and corners just as the deeds describe."

Astute Public Servants

IN ONE OF THE very small towns within my usual territory, a Mr. and Mrs. Jones, devoted citizens and public benefactors, had taken a special interest in the improvement and beautification of the cemetery. After another public-spirited man had donated some adjoining land for its enlargement, the Joneses had the entire tract—old part and new—enclosed by a fine new wall built by the most noted stone mason of the region. The town's gratitude for all this was appropriately expressed on a bronze plate on one side of the stone entrance gateway.

Mr. Jones died before the completion of the project, but Mrs. Jones had wished to take care of what work remained, which consisted mainly of laying out the new, unoccupied part of the graveyard in four-by-eleven-foot individual burial plots and making a map to show this plan. I was employed by the cemetery commissioners to do the work.

After making a survey and preliminary map for the commissioners, I staked out and then showed on the map a proper and logical division of as many individual plots as seemed necessary. Those parts of the new yard which seemed difficult to incorporate into any logical extension of the system, were left blank.

I showed the map in tentative pencil form to the commissioners for their consideration. Their spokesman said, "We would like to have you go ahead and divide and stake off *all* the land now."

I pointed out to him the difficulty of doing that, and said that, in view of the very gradual rate at which the cemetery was being taken up, he could easily see that I had already laid out enough plots to last for the next seventy-five or a hundred years. I added the further suggestion that the problems of what to do after that could safely be left to posterity.

"You may be right," he said. "But you see, Mr. Chase, if that work is done now, during Mrs. Jones' lifetime, she will pay for it."

A President, Anyhow

FOLLOWING a well-attended church service in East Alstead one Sunday, there was a business meeting. While such a good number was thus gathered, several members took the occasion to suggest that various former customs, recently fallen into disuse, be once more revived—making the church seem more like the good old times.

Lyle Kemp, a life-long resident and devoted member, rose to express his strong desire that the yoke of the church bell—a genuine Revere—be repaired; it had been out of order for a year or two. Although it could rarely be heard at his farm, two miles to the north, still he missed the thought of its regular and inspiring Sunday morning call to worship. And especially did he miss the gentle tolling of the bell—always rung in the past—as an accompaniment to the pastor's mounting of the pulpit. So eloquent was he in urging the repair of the bell yoke and our return to its time-honored uses, and so enthusiastic were the many expressions of agreement, that at first we did not notice that Mary Cutting, one of our very oldest members, was standing up, and trying—in a weak and tremulous but deeply perturbed voice—to make herself heard.

At last recognized by the moderator, Mary was of course then given the attention of the meeting. She expressed great regret at feeling impelled to object, on purely personal grounds, to a suggestion that appeared to have the unanimous support of all others. But there was a side to this she could not overlook.

"To hear the bell tolled as you suggest," she said with much emotion, "would always be a very painful reminder to me." Struggling to control her voice, and leaning with trembling

126

hands on the back of the next bench, she explained her over-powering feelings.

"The last time I heard a church bell tolled was on the sad occasion of the death of our honored president, Calvin Coolidge. . . . If I heard those solemn tones again, that sad loss to our country would be brought back to me most forcefully."

Her impassioned plea of objection then tapered off weakly into dejected silence as she started to sit down.

But she straightened up again, impelled by an afterthought, expressed in a tone of some doubt: "Or perhaps it was President Harding."

Alstead: The Priceless Parish

I HAVE SERVED on several pulpit committees for the cooperating Congregational churches of our town. At the meetings we could always count on Francis Pratt, the Center's regular representative, to liven things up with down-to-earth practicality, time-tested wise slogans, and sly humor.

The spirit of such meetings can well use some of these qualities. Every mature member knows that to find a new pastor, who can happily satisfy the varied desires of three rural congregations, avoid all the errors of his predecessor, and be universally liked, approved of, and supported by young and old alike, can be next to impossible.

On one occasion we were gathered at a house in the Village to meet and consider the tentative candidacy of one John Van Blarcom, then visiting several parishes in our vicinity. The visit and discussion had been unusually pleasant and hopeful. Aside from the one or two participants who, because of cynicism or timidity, habitually remained silent on such occasions, all seemed pleased with the candidate and much in favor of "extending him a call."

Finally, Francis, taking it upon himself to speak the common mind, leaned forward, extended his hands in a gesture of earnest welcome, and said, "Mr. Van Blarcom, will you come?"

This may have represented our general feelings, yet I was sure that others must agree with me that the question was a bit premature. Thinking to spare our guest any possible embarrassment, I said, "I think we would respect this man more if he were to take plenty of time to think over our proposition."

"No!" said Francis, swinging toward me. "That's wrong! . . . He who hesitates is lost!"

128

Elm City

Keene, New Hampshire

THE KEENE SUMMER THEATRE, during its successful years, was carried on as a true "labor of love" by Beatrice Booth Colony (of the famous Booth theatrical family) and her husband, Alfred Taylor Colony. She was the director, and both of them frequently appeared in the cast. They are now at rest, and, unfortunately—as in enterprises largely carried on by the energy and devotion of the original founders—this one did not long survive those who started it.

Like many summer theatres, this one was housed in a big old barn, and was located on the farm where Mr. Colony had spent his boyhood. As he and I stood chatting, well before curtain time one lovely evening, on the lawn between the barn and the large, square, aristocratic white house that was still his home, he remarked to me with a smile, "I'll tell you, the noises that come from that barn now are some different from the sound of the pigs that were kept there when I was a boy!"

Once I took two young ladies—both with a deep love of theatre and some professional experience—to attend a performance there. During the evening one of them became interested in joining the cast for the following year. I offered to introduce her to Mrs. Colony after the play.

We were most warmly welcomed into the brightly lighted, southeast parlor of the big house, where Mrs. Colony was happy to relax and visit with her patrons—her evening's work now over. She entertained us most graciously as she gave full play to her life-long devotion to the world of the stage. She spoke of the various joys and sorrows, successes and failures.

She spoke especially of *Lady Windemere's Fan*—"the very essence of drama" in her feeling—a play in which she had once acted and with which she had hoped to end the current season. But then, her voice and spirit subdued by consideration of the unavoidable business side of running a theatre, she revealed sadly that the plan had been given up. The season was to end with *The Moon is Blue*, and she seemed to recoil dramatically from the mere utterance of the name.

"Do you know the play?" she fervently asked as she glanced from one to the other of us for sympathy.

My companion did, and they shared a mutual regret that the company should be forced to such a come-down in artistic and dramatic taste by the grimy dictates of the "box office."

Throwing out her hands in a gesture of despair, our hostess said, "Friends, what more can be said?—Keene is a *manufacturing* town!"

The Real Trouble

THERE HAVE BEEN many ways in the past of expressing the idea
that this would be a great world if it were not for the people. And
ever new ways will, no doubt, be found in the future.

George Robertson lived at Downer's Corner, Weathersfield,
Vermont, for nearly half a century. In his old age he spent much
of the time in his rocking chair on the southeast corner of the
porch of his old, two-story farmhouse, which stood not over
fifty feet from the intersection of State Routes 106 and 131. He
could recall the successive changes and improvements that had
evolved in these two increasingly busy arteries of travel. From
dirt and mud lanes, in the days of the ox and the horse, the
carriage and the wagon, the sled and the sleigh and the Model T
Ford, they had become paved, broad-shouldered, "through"
highways with "engineered" alignments and grades. From
his perfect vantage point, George could watch the growing
volume and speed of modern traffic in this nervous, impatient,
hairbreadth, competitive age.

Late one day in early fall my assistant and I joined him on the
porch, introduced ourselves, and received his gruff but cheerful
welcome and the offer of chairs. I told him our purpose in coming
again to the "Corner"—to check details of highway signs, widths,
and distances for a court map in a case involving a collision at
this intersection a year or so before. Oh, yes, he had surmised
what we had been up to the day before, when he had seen us
surveying the roads for several hundred feet in all four directions.
And it had brought back to his mind the collision scene, enacted
before his very eyes. He waxed vehement recalling the event: who
the parties were, which way each had been travelling and where
each had ended up after the crash—and in what condition.

131

In the early dusk of this warm evening, our conversation was interspersed by periods of silence; each of us absorbed in his own thoughts, as we gazed at the steady but intermittent flow of cars and trucks moving in all four directions, some driving straight through, others turning to right or left. The change of work shifts at the plants in Springfield and Windsor, though fifteen miles or so to the south and east, was largely responsible for these regular tidal waves of traffic at this hour, even at a rural corner this far away.

Watching the scene, we exchanged observations from time to time on the temperaments of the various drivers; their care or lack of it. Most adhered to the letter and spirit of the law, but a certain proportion would break it with infractions, great or small, crowding their luck, imposing on the alertness of others.

From our vantage point it was apparent that every oncoming driver, even a total stranger to the area, was well warned in advance of a hazardous intersection; on each of the four approaches the highway department had done all it could to reduce danger by placing warning signs 250 yards away. But to what effect? The great improvements in roads; the competition among carmakers to produce greater horsepower and running smoothness; the habitual impatience of Americans—have all combined in a relentless tendency for the forces of modern times to outgrow the simplicity and onetime charm of an unguarded, unregulated rural corner such as "Downer's." They have created at such points a constant percentage of hazard unknown half a century ago. Then, if conscience or honor were not necessarily less lacking than today, at least the rarity of any motor vehicle on the road, the slowness and small volume of traffic, and the rough roads usually acted to confine accidents to such events as "locked" carriage wheels, runaway horses, overturned "potato bug" sleighs, and broken axles.

And so, as we sat on the porch that warm summer evening, gazing at the crossroads scene, this particular accident I had just finished surveying seemed—in the perspective of our collective thoughts—entirely predictable in the statistical sense, mankind being what it is.

Toward the end of the visit, and breaking one of our silent

contemplations of the procession, the Sage of Downer's Corner embraced in a few well-chosen words the substance of his own conclusions: "I tell you, Mr. Chase, the trouble today is the God damned public."

Spring Idyl

Dedicated to Perley Swett, the hermit
of Stoddard, New Hampshire, and to William P. House,
forester, of Chesham, New Hampshire

On a bright and sunny day in early spring
When birds their welcome songs began to sing,
While yet upon the road lay snow and ice,
We met the Hermit of Devil's Paradise.

This appellation he had thought of as his own;
A hermit, it is true, he lived alone.
But though the light of Paradise was in this spot,
Dread darkness of the Evil One, I thought, was not.

Over a long and tortuous route we came,
A road of the earliest settlers,
A hundred years the same,
Winding around or over
The stubborn features of terrain
Within the ancient right-of-way stone walls,
Past former clearings, cellar holes,
And private, beckoning lanes,
Reminding us of earlier, better days
And former, self-reliant, now abandoned, ways
Of settlers' teeming, rural life—
Man's transient conquest, long ago,
In his and Nature's strife—
Where all is silent now, resigned,
Amid the forest's stealthy but inexorable return,
To Nature's re-assertion of herself.

Imperceptably at first, but ever stronger growing,
Did the peace, the silence,
And the dead past's memory
Ascend to wrap us in its wonder,
To gratify and haunt us many days.

Some points were landmarks
We should be concerned with later on—
Wall corners, brooklets, road forks and the like—
That we made mental note of,
As now and then we halted, getting breath,
With compass, maps, and documents in hand.

Pressing on and ever eastward,
Far ahead we heard the voice
Most typical of Spring's resurgent life:
Tumultuous waters
Released from Winter's bondage, joyous to be free,
Gregariously starting the long journey to the sea.
They rushed beneath the bridge;
We had to raise our voices some
To speak of this as one more mark.

Crossing this we came out in the open
Where the warm, late-morning sun
Had thawed the snow and ice and mud,
And started little hurrying streamlets
Down the rutted wheel tracks of the road.

Curving to northward, finally, up ahead,
We saw the present home and birthplace—
Low-posted, ancient farm house,
Sheds and wood piles, barns and all—
Of him who called this region "Paradise."

When Winter's grip should weaken in the spring
He had long expected us to come,
To find and mark and map the bounds of forest lands—
Lands that on many lines adjoined his own.

135

No special day had been agreed upon,
Yet, as we gained the yard,
Why, there he was! framed in an eastern doorway,
Gazing out upon his own domain
As if contemplating what the day might bring.
Then seeing us, he raised his hand,
Marked the good weather we had brought, and asked us in.

We entered, by custom of the country,
Through the shed, past indoor well-curb,
Stove wood neatly piled, and miscellaneous mass
Of well-worn tools, the broken parts of harnesses—
In short, unnumbered relics of the
Ways and means of "Candle Days."

Our eyes, accustomed to the morning's brightness,
Found the dim interior dark, as, in the room most used
And finding seats at his direction,
We settled by the kitchen stove.

In here there seemed a sense of History's long reach,
From Bible times up to this very year.
Our host took his accustomed place
Before a window to the north where the reflected glare
From settling drifts outside would silhouette
His head with bushy rim of hair and beard.
Two goats, from his flock of sixty-odd outside,
Kept in for special care, were clamoring for attention,
Trying to mount the barrier in a doorway
To a darkened room beyond. And trampled underfoot
Lay a torn and grimy front-page scrap
That headlined "Gaza Strip" and "Crop Control"—
Two jarring and discordant notes, to me
Whose mind sought orientation, finding peace,
Here, in this place: a veritable confluence
Of varied ages, lives, and viewpoints
Yet of understanding and relaxed good will.

The gracious master of this house, unknown before, to me,
Was an isolated remnant of a past community,
Yielding but little to abandonment's adversity.
He was alone the region's spokesman, offering its welcome,
His its gentle voice and only vocal memory—
Sole supplement to written records and the
Silent, enigmatic patterns of the walls, marked trees,
And stone piles we must learn to comprehend.

I turned, responding to his introductory pleasantries—
About the weather, and "mud time" it would shortly bring,
And what the traveling would then be like—
And to his host's concession, offered for our benefit:
His genial reference to the distance this must seem,
To us, from civilization.
Had he thus thought to guess our minds, he was in error;
This was a welcome respite from our usual world:
That world, which, "late and soon" is "too much with us."
The distance of any such fell stage in Mankind's life,
For us, for a time, could well remain.

He brought out verses, written by himself,
Reflective of sly humor and of independent thought,
Describing, too, the frontier manners and the vicious acts
Of various travelers far from home,
Caught off their courteous or their moral guard:
Goats shot for deer, left dead upon the frozen earth,
The theft of Christmas trees for the hollow empty shell
Of celebration of the Savior's birth.

He brought out maps, drawn by himself,
Piecing together records from the county seat
And his own observations of the landmarks round about.
He would accompany us, he said,
For any help that he might give;
To see, also, if we, by deeds and scientific means
Might prove or disprove

Judgments long but tentatively held by him.
Any discrepancies could amicably be resolved,
He felt quite sure.
And in the days to come this proved the case.

Through wood and pasture, brush and swamp,
By pond shore, brooklet, wall and road,
With compass, rod, and "chain", bush knife and axe,
Ten days in "Paradise" we spent with him.

Mostly we had all Nature to ourselves,
For work, for thought, for fellowship.
When we ceased work and speech, and sat a while,
On snow-cleared rock or fallen tree,
For rest and absorption of the solitude,
At times there was a stillness in the air
So near to absolute silence as to be believed
Only by efforts to detect a single sound.
And once some tiny bird up in a tree,
Who must have seen us though we saw not him,
Twittered in such a high, small voice
That it seemed he must be but one inch long!
But when he stopped the intensity of the silence
Again approached the absolute.

And then there were the long stone walls,
Built by the earliest settlers
In all similar rural regions,
In clearing land and fencing stock,
And giving notice to the world
This hard-earned land was theirs!

There had been plenty of material for that work,
For, of all the many places used by the world's Creator
As a dumping ground, this certainly was one
For scattering stones left over when His work was done!

There would have been but intermittent silence
In those days of building wall;
The stalwart farmer was there then, with sons and teams,
With stone boat, pick and shovel, bars and chains,
Joined at times by their abutting neighbors
For big days along the common boundary lines,
With a loud and forward-looking sociability
While there lurked, ever in the minds of all,
Cool jugs, brought by the girls and women,
Set out of danger in the shade.

That was a part of how early settlers put down roots;
This is where they were destined to sojourn
Alas but for one short century, then to start leaving
For indoor lives in cities and "Satanic mills"
Or easier tilling of the western plains.

Each of such contemplations of the past would end
In awakening to the need of pressing on.
Weather and all conditions of the footing
Held just long enough;
The solid, settled snow bridged us from rock to rock,
While on the pond, whose shore must be traversed,
The rotting ice of spring accommodated us
Yet we were warned—by openings at its very edge
And muted gurglings of streamlets come to life—
To haste the final measurements and compass sights.

It is good when recreation and vocation coincide;
Thus, as a last embellishment and self-expressive act,
To the graphic record of our work we put our message
To the generations yet to come, which was where road
And town line intersect, marked unmistakably
With white, exotic marble, brought a hundred miles.

After the end of our last day, we took our leave
With thanks and warm regards, and with the further sense
That fellowship and vivid memories would never fade;
Also that, when from all true men and objects they pursue

Is winnowed out the chaff, there will be found
Beneath the screen, something from "Paradise"
Touching the mind and heart of Judgment
To survive the fateful day.

Into our conscious minds the modern world
Then broke with a typical sign unfurled,
A symbol of Mankind's contemplation
And quest of a misconceived salvation:

Streaking from south to north and turning
Eastward to meet the night returning,
Long vapor trails, in order, silent and high,
Plowed the darkening sunset sky.

Like the Birds

THE LAST DAYS OF Gene Hodskin's losing struggle for life were a busy and anxious time for his family, relatives, friends and neighbors. He was well liked by everyone, and there was a constant coming and going in the farm house yard of all those who wished to give help or comfort in any way possible. Those most capable of meeting the needs took turns at the steady vigil of sick-room sitting, day and night. There was plenty of help around the house and barns; Gene's brother-in-law could always think of just the right words for assuring Gene—in his conscious moments—that all the animals had just been well watered and fed.

There were few if any "wonder drugs" in those days. If perchance a middle aged person survived pneumonia, it was less likely to have been due to straight medicine than to the doctor's long familiarity with the patient and his family, their medical history and ways of living, and his own art or instinct—and rare fortune! Dr. P. B. Stevens had long been the physician and devoted friend of the family, and was in steady attendance all during this trying ordeal.

Mrs. Ida Burroughs, Gene's mother-in-law, and mother of nine grown sons and daughters all raised on the nearby Burroughs farm, had seen much of life, and life had well prepared her for her role on this occasion; all about the kitchen, sitting room, and sick-chamber, she was a tower of calm courage, strength, perspective, and consolation.

One of the rich summer people, in her big, chauffeur-driven, Peerless touring car, came to express her sincere sympathy and concern. Regrettably, her call was longest remembered for her unsolicited admonition regarding medical talent.

"Is the doctor doing everything that he should?" she asked.

Mrs. Burroughs, with faithful appreciation of Dr. Stevens' earnest efforts, said, "We are sure he is doing the very best he can."

Then the visitor said, "Well, if he didn't do just what I thought he should, I would cast him aside and get someone who would!" And with that, she entered her car and rode away.

As Mrs. Burroughs watched them start down the road, she remarked, "Some of these summer people! They come and flutter around for a while like the birds, and then they're gone."

A Misconceived Stand Backfires

NEAR HANCOCK, NEW HAMPSHIRE, on a trip home one summer
day, I decided to call on Peter Garland, a young architect, to
ask about progress on an interesting project of his for which I
had recently done some work.

My knock at the door of their country place brought his wife
and one of the children. Mrs. Garland, a tall, slim, and very
attractive blonde young woman, explained that her husband
was away for the day.

On a previous visit there, I had seen what a pleasant and
intelligent young couple they were, devoted to each other and
to their two very young children—altogether a pleasing family
indeed. So—with the appreciation one naturally feels at the
prospect of a "happy event"—I noticed that before many more
weeks another little Garland would be welcomed into the world.

I left my best wishes and was soon on my way, thinking of
other things.

Rounding a sharp turn in the winding country road I
suddenly had to slow down, for just ahead was an old lady with
a wire-haired terrier straining at the leash. I stopped to chat as
soon as I saw that it was the Garlands' neighbor, Miss Margaret
Perry, who had so kindly entertained my helper and myself on the
day of the survey for Mr. Garland. It had been very hot that day,
and she had graciously invited us into her cool basement living
room for a rest and some cold refreshmants. It was a most
pleasant room, with an elegant old Chickering grand piano,
numerous oil paintings she had done, and other indications of
her cultural propensities. I learned too that we had both been
brought up in the same very proper Boston suburb, where she
still spent the winters.

But now, standing at the roadside with her dog and recognizing me, she said, "Why Mr. Chase, how do you do? Well, are you doing some more surveying out this way?"

"No", I said. "I just went out to see Mr. Garland".

"Well, you couldn't have found him at home; this is one of the days he teaches, down at Smith College".

"I know", I said. "Mrs. Garland was there and told me so".

After some solicitous attentions to the dog, again straining at the leash, she said, "I suppose you know they're going to have another child."

Now this remark caught me off guard, and posed a question: To know or not to know? But there was no time for a conscious, calculated decision without arousing her suspicion of my straightforwardness. It must have been some reflex of instinct—misguided as it proved—that caused me to say what I did. I shall never be able fully to explain it; I am a family man, and the "facts of life" have always been simply the facts, like any others.

Anyhow, with an affected air of non-concern calculated to end the matter, I merely said, "I don't know anything about it".

But this did not end the matter. She asked incredulously, "Didn't you say you had just come from there?"

"Yes, sure".

"And you say you didn't know?"

Was there no way out of this? Could I pretend not to have heard her? No, she stood close to the car window and knew I was not deaf. Oh! if only another car had come along just then and honked for the right of way! Or if I could have been driving a horse, who mercifully for me might just then have been attacked by yellow jackets! But alas, no such rescue was to be. I felt like the victim of a summer afternoon's prank of the Gods, who, in a jolly mood, had sprung on me a trap set by myself. All Nature seemed to listen, to miss not a single word by which I might try to escape.

There was no turning back, of course; now irrevocably committed to a certain stand, I had passed the "point of no return". So, with all the tone of indifference and finality I could possibly muster in one last, desperate effort to close the matter on my own terms, I said again, "I don't know anything about it".

She stepped back from the car, looked off for a moment, then said, with an air of resignation, "Well, perhaps men don't notice such things".

144

To the Last

George H. Duncan, 1876-1958

As a LIFE-LONG DEVOTEE of the philosophy of Henry George,
George Duncan, with his rich sense of humor, his endless stock
of economic illustrations from real life, and his broad experience
in politics and human living, was indeed the type of man best
fitted to "win friends and influence people"—in marked contrast
with many, more pedantic devotees of that philosophy!

When anyone professes dedication to human betterment
through some specific reform, it is only natural to ask what his
motives are and his ideas of handling individual people and
society during whatever he envisions as an inevitable transi-
tional period.

The theory as a whole must be judged to some extent by the
people adhering to it and by the ways in which they have treated
other people in the past and propose to treat them while bringing
in some new regime in the future. Can they good-naturedly
tolerate some degree of compromise so as to get along successfully with others? Do they have a real sense of humor, one of the
truest proofs of having a sense of proportion? Can they recog-
nize the rights of those who may disagree? If not, then they, as
prospective mid-wives for a better society, cannot be trusted, and
their basic theory may be suspect as well.

In the light of all this, I like to think of George Duncan as
having been an advocate of Henry George's philosophy of the
very highest order, a most admirable representative, and personally worthy of faith, trust, and respect.

George had a quality greatly lacking in most public "leader-
ship" today: a broad sense of reality. He had held about every
public office in New Hampshire except governor; he had worked
some years in Washington politics as secretary to a senator; had
traveled, read, lectured and studied widely always, and was

indeed a true sophisticate in economics and politics, yet for many years ran a small-town drugstore, and, on his own land set out many thousands of pine seedlings (now a stand of considerable value) many of them "with these two hands", as he expressed it.

Such breadth of experience contributes to validity of viewpoint and opinion in a man basically loving and intellectually active.

George had an understanding sympathy for every man and his natural desire to get ahead in any legitimate way available to him. If sin or injustice to others or to society, openly condoned by laws or customs, were thus involved, it would be these that he would condemn and seek to reform, not the individual profiting by them. On many occasions during our travels, telling me of this or that particularly notorious case of land speculation, usually lucrative, he would end by saying "Of course you can't blame him!"

He was always ready with his famous story of how he got his first lesson in the economics of taxation. At an early age he was elected to the board of three selectmen in his home town of Jaffrey. One day in early April during "mud time", he and the other two selectmen drove out in a horse and carriage to assess property for taxation. One farmer had, among other items, one hog in excess of the number regularly exempted. Reaching a final agreement as to which one to tax and at what valuation took over an hour's time for the four able-bodied men thus involved. In the end they determined a tax of six cents to be collected later by the town. He said, "That day I began to question if this manner of taxation was entirely practical".

Because of his warmth of friendly feeling toward other people and his rich sense of humor, he was always great fun to be with. Rather than expressing monotonous condemnation of all the world's crazy ideas and customs, he found much amusement at their expense. He always enjoyed recalling the one we heard in the subway station in Cambridge under Harvard Square—the idea that unemployment must be accepted as a fixed factor in life. Of course the same idea has been accepted and expressed with great verbosity on higher levels of intellectual circles but surely with no greater clarity than on this occasion. Since we were on our way to a class dinner at the Boston branch of the Henry

George School of Social Science and full of old "homecoming" spirit, we were in a good mood to appreciate what we heard. Waiting for our train we had made small purchases at the concession stand. I drew off the wrapper of my five-cent Hershey bar and looked around for a waste basket. The saleslady, noticing, said, "Just throw it on the floor, Mister." "Oh, I hate to do that", I said. "That's all right, Mister," she said, "Makes a job for somebody."

Then there was the time he used me as a sad, hypothetical example. It was one winter when I was teaching classes in Henry George's *Progress and Poverty* at the library in Keene, New Hampshire, and he was doing the same in the Congregational Church in Peterborough. I was visiting his class one evening. Glancing about for a newcomer in the audience, to illustrate a point, George said, "Now let's take Mr. Chase here. We'll say he comes to town, a lonely stranger, and, like so many, he spends an evening in a bar, drinks a little too much, starts away but falls in a ditch; is taken in by the police and next day fined fifteen dollars for disorderly conduct. Soon he buys an old house and starts to fix it up. The taxes had previously been a certain amount. He cleans up the yard and paints the house, to the great improvement of the looks of his street, gaining everyone's approval including that of the selectmen. Next year his taxes are raised fifteen dollars. Asking those men the reason for this, he is told it is because he has improved his place and made it worth more. Then he recalls that that was just what it had cost him the time he got drunk. This is liable to leave him in a state of confusion. How's he going to know which they prefer? or which was the greater offense? After he had paid his fine for disorderliness they had been willing to forget it. But not his improvements! For these they will "fine" him year after year. We can only hope that brooding over this will not lead to a repetition of the first offense."

And finally, there was the matter of his own funeral service. Again, as it happened, we were on a trip to Boston. In the subway he told me how he had been working on plans for his last official recognition on this earth—where it was to be held, and for what reasons; how selected friends, (who had best understood and shared his deepest beliefs as to "man's rela-

147

tionship to Mother Earth and his fellows") were to be asked to take part. We were just coming up on to the Charles River bridge when I said, "I certainly hope Henry George will be mentioned." Symbolically, as it has always seemed to me since, we reached the highest point of the bridge over the center of the river, in the bright, late afternoon sun, when George gave his reply: "Oh yes, he will be; you don't think I'm going to die for nothing, do you?" And then for one short moment, the drab placidity of other passengers' faces was disturbed, their glances (some with a slight smile of wonderment) turning toward us as there rang out one loud, long peal of that joyous laughter so unique to George Duncan alone—a most happy sound that will ever echo down the halls of as much time as any of his friends shall live.

An Effort to be Accurate

I WAS ONCE asked to survey a shore cottage lot belonging to two women, and on reaching the lake, I stopped at a tiny grocery store to ask the way. The cheerful, little old proprietor was at once very happy to be of service, with information both useful and, as I realized later, discerning.

"Do I know Annie and Hattie?" he said. "Oh, sure! For years and years I know Annie and Hattie. Oh, yes. Very, very nice ladies."

He gave directions to their place.

But then, still wishing to be as friendly and helpful as he could, and to be certain I would get off to a good start with these old neighbors of his, he added:

"Now, Mister, it is Annie that you want to deal with. She's the one that really knows the lot. And you will know which one she is all right. She's big and tall, wears overalls and a man's cap; she smokes cigarettes and struts around exactly like a man. Well, perhaps not exactly. But you'll see. I tell you what: she looks just like a cross between a man and a woman!"

Disappointment at the Court House

AT THE BEAUTIFUL old Windham County Court House at Newfane, a Vermont farmer and his wife sat in the Plaintiff's Room with their attorney and four witnesses. The early June morning was most enchanting; the fresh, cool air of early summer and the songs of birds came in the open windows, and all in the room were feeling sociable and relaxed, chatting about all manner of irrelevant things, waiting for the opening of the morning session. There would be no nerve strain, worry or hard feelings in this case, which was simply that of an owner trying to get more compensation for land of his to be taken for a highway relocation than the State had, up to now, offered.

There came an urgent knock at the door, and a messenger told the farmer's attorney he was wanted in "Judge's Chambers". He went, but in a very few minutes he was back. Closing the door behind him, he said, "Henry, the State has just made a final offer of fifteen-hundred dollars (an amount over fifty percent greater than previously offered). "Now, you could accept that figure and end the whole case right this minute; or, if you still want to go into court and try to get more, we'll do that. You're the boss and it's up to you. It is not for me to urge you one way or the other, but let me say that as a friend I'd advise you to accept it."

In an attitude of inner turmoil and indecision Henry ran his fingers through his hair, and after some hesitation and a deep sigh, said, "Well, now I don't know about that. Seems like they could just as well . . ." Turning to his wife he said, "What do you say about this?" She started to ask about a number of minor considerations—something about the tractor, perhaps, or one of their cows. Wearily, the attorney began shaking his head, any such matters were now out of the question; the seconds were

150

fast slipping away. He put his hand on the stub of the missing door knob and, starting to turn it, said "Folks, you will simply have to make up your minds; I have got to give the judge an answer right away."

Henry stalled around a minute more in a desperate delaying action of backward thoughts and jumbled mutterings. Of course he might have been trying to refrain from rubbing his hands briskly under the table, for all any of those present might have known. Finally, leaning back in his chair with an air of sad resignation he said, "Well, I s'pose we'll have to take it. Yes, I guess that's the best we can do. We'll do what you say . . . But you know, Mr. Lowery, I'm awful disappointed in one way. All this time I've been looking forward to seeing you in action in the court room."

An Evening with Scott Nearing

"To live fully . . . the individual . . . must reach beyond self."
—S. N., 1972

IN ABOUT 1920, with other members of our Pennsylvania prep-school debating team, I went to New York to hear Scott Nearing in Cooper Union Hall in a debate with some other man not now recalled.

During the train ride back, we agreed that Mr. Nearing had "wiped up the floor" with his opponent. To us school boys—altruistic, socially concerned, and trained in the ideals of Quakerism—he had suddenly become a realistic and articulate hero in the cause of common humanity—as opposed to the greed, pleadings, and opportunism of private, powerful "special interests" and the bias, isolationism, and irrelevancy of the academic world. And ever since that day, just the very name "Scott Nearing" has invariably cast a magic spell over my consciousness, even to this day.

I wish I might have become better acquainted with him in the immediately ensuing years. Perhaps the unbridged gap between the respective philosophies of Marx (or other socialists, or communists, or leftists, or whatever) and of Henry George might always have stood between us in some measure. But judging by what I now picture as the subsequent courses of our lives, I think that gap could have been allowed to rest. We both grew in the active desire to live at peace with Nature, God, and Man, honestly, simply, and with due regard for the rights of all others, present and future, to do the same.

Many years later I was to meet Scott and Helen Nearing when they lived in Vermont, and I called on them several times on the way home from surveying trips in the region of Dorset and Manchester. They had established an organic farm and built their own buildings themselves in an out-of-the-way district of the rural town of Jamaica, after Scott had gotten tired of city life and had quit struggling with the "establishment" in his former fields of teaching, lecturing, and writing.

The Nearings—he alone or with Helen—have written a vast number and variety of books, articles, pamphlets, and so forth, on social questions. They have travelled through every state of this country and nearly every country of the world, especially where history was being made. With their broad and varied background of travel and study, they are indeed entitled to feel they know what they are talking about on world social affairs, because they can truly say "We have been there and seen for ourselves"—a solidly valid viewpoint. There is, we must admit, a tendency for critics of life to see what they are looking for, all too often the vindication of beliefs already held. That could apply to them and to me, as well. While the Nearings would most likely see evidence in all countries of the evils of private enterprise and "monopoly capitalism", I, as an adherent of Henry George, would see evidence of land monopoly and speculation. (And we might both be right!)

In any event, however different our conclusions might be, there would still be no spiritual barrier between us, for, I believe, we share a common motivation: the earnest desire for justice and peace and the willingness to exert ourselves to those ends.

The Nearings would probably claim that they had attained a life far simpler and closer to Nature than I. And they would be right. But I would remind them that many such matters are relative; they once poked fun at one of their neighbors, in my hearing, for living in a primitive, back-woods way a few hundred yards up a woods-road branch off their own, very rural road!

The Nearings have had considerable influence on my thinking. they would be glad to know. Two instances are worth recalling.

I learned—never mind how!—that Scott did not want a lawn mower on the place. Later, when I asked him why, he said, "Because it is just one more thing to have to be made, bought, paid for, maintained, and housed. The fewer such mechanical things a man has, the better." I gave that answer much careful consideration, and since that very day I have thought twice before I bought any tool, machine, or other "thing", asking myself if I really needed it, or wanted to devote the time and energy it would require to buy and maintain it. Often it resulted in not taking on some additional encumbrance.

When I was writing my book on American ideals, and while attempting to define differing schools of economic philosophy, I defined socialism in terms of what I thought were, or would be, its results, failing to define its elements of organization as proposed by its adherents. I got a swift come-back from the Nearings, and deserved it. We did not have a true "meeting of minds" by any means, in our exchange of words. But I suddenly realized that before you make an analysis of any philosophy or school of thought, you must first state its principals and substance as a true and informed adherent would state them. Being taken to task as I was, was a good lesson. I realized I was new to the field of philosophical criticism, and shall ever be grateful that the Nearings pulled no punches.

Though I have not seen Scott or Helen since they moved to Maine, I have had some of their books and read articles about them. I feel a growing loyalty, respect, and affection for them— because of their championing the rights and best interests of all people everywhere, as they see them; because of their example in cutting out so many of the material and unnecessary trappings of conventional society so as to allow time for reading, study, music, travel, and searching conversation—life's ultimate ends in themselves—; and because of their active respect and love for our natural environment—their exemplary lives, in other words— pointing the way toward peace and permanency, and growth of the inner, individual personality. And therefore, it does my heart good to see them, in this changing age, "coming into their own" by numerous important phases of their actual way of life at last being recognized as vital to the very continued life of humanity.

Society in general—or its thinking membership, at least—is at last waking up to the tragedies of our future if we continue to destroy our resources and degrade our collective life by tyranny, exploitation, war, ostentatious living, and phlegmatic personal habits. So it is indeed natural that people should "discover" the Nearings who have already been practicing for years the very principles of life so recently realized as basic to "The Way Ever-lasting."

Only Scott himself could possibly do justice to his own remarkable story, which he has done in *The Making of a Radical*, the fascinating autobiography of America's most notable present-day socialist. Though he fails to clearly define his key word, "radical", and though I am no socialist, yet I am deeply impressed by this story of a life-long and courageous dedication and self-sacrificing struggle for a better social order—as he has conceived that to be.

Though all my visits at the Nearing place in Vermont are now treasured memories, the last is best recalled.

Scott greeted me at the door and invited me to stay to supper if I thought I could eat "what we are going to have." Recalling that "beggars can't be choosers" and to meet the challenge to sportsmanship he so cheerfully extended, I gave him the only possible rejoinder: "I'll try anything once." "Then we shall be glad to have you stay", he said.

In the kitchen I was introduced to two men who obviously were working on supper preparations. One sat at a table, cutting up vegetables or fruit of some kind; the other was operating some sort of buzzing little machine on the kitchen counter. Scott explained that it was a carrot grinder and dejuicer. He said we were going to have a drink of carrot juice, and then croquettes made of the solids and baked.

After we had chatted a few minutes we sat silently for a time.

My coming, I was then to learn, had evidently interrupted an earnest conversation on social philosophy—very typical in that household. The dialogue that then occurred might seem insignificant if taken outside of the context of the whole emphasis of the Nearings' life work; I would never have remembered it at all—word for word, as I do—had it not been such a brief but revealing gem of philosophical tenacity.

The man at the table laid down his knife, turned toward our host, and said, "But Scott, can't you realize that there could be injustice and corruption under any system of social organization?"

As if wishing to drop the matter for the time being, Scott

turned just a little away in his chair, looked toward the floor, and apparently with deep reluctance, softly said but one word: "Perhaps".

During the ensuing moments of silence—but for the buzzing little grinder—the man at the table resumed his work and I got up to stroll into the living room.

Since electric lights are so nearly universal, their recent installation at Nearings had escaped my notice at first and the full realization came only when I started walking around. I quickly stepped back to the kitchen and said, "Why Scott, you've been electrified! Aren't you slipping?"

"That was my wife's idea", he said.

"Oh. By the way, where is Helen tonight?"

"Over in Manchester, visiting her sister."

Glancing at the electric grinder, still buzzing away merrily, and at all the bright lights in living room, kitchen and entry, I said, "Well, in her absence you certainly seem to be making pretty generous use of the electricity."

Unable to escape the implication of my observations, Scott faced the situation honestly—and with a candid remark that all of us might very well heed.

With an air of resignation and due humility, he said, "That's the trouble with all such modern things; you get used to them and then you can't leave them alone."

On the Surveying Business

AN OLD NEIGHBOR, Rob Squibb, a Harvard man, later a teacher of Latin in several private schools, now long retired to our pleasant town, once said that he would like to help me on any surveying jobs not too long or strenuous. I liked the idea, and I harbored the thought that the experience might impress Rob with the importance, the dignity, the lofty economic and social status of surveying as one of society's most vital callings.

On our first trip we drove twelve miles or so up to a farm where I had been requested to measure off and describe a small parcel of land our client said her parents were giving her out of the old family place where she had grown up.

On our arrival at the old farmhouse, loud shouting and arguing could be heard inside. Finally a young woman, our client, saw that we were there and came out. She said, "I am sorry to tell you that there will be no surveying after all. My parents have gone back on their promise. . . . But of course I wish to pay you for your time and trouble coming up." Five dollars was agreed to—very little, but in my practice, dealing directly with people personally, it is always natural to offer to share the misfortumes of life.

That was that. We returned to Rob's place, and said Goodnight as the shadows were lengthening, the afternoon gone.

The second occasion was in another direction.

An old lady in Keene called to say that she wanted me to come right away, to settle a land dispute which had been going on for fifteen years but which I, as a surveyor, could settle in five minutes. When I doubted that any such quick settlement could be expected, she launched such a challenge to my manhood and my status as a surveyor that my curiosity got the best of me, and in the end I realized I had said I would come.

Rob agreed to go on this trip, and on the way down, after being informed of the controversial nature of the work in prospect, said, "Well then, you can do the talking."

On reaching the place, I urged Rob to come in, as the discussion might be interesting. "No sir!", said Rob. "You just leave me out of this".

Inside, the old lady asked me to sit down, and then said, "Young man. (I was about forty-five at the time) I want you to untie the knot".

When I asked what she meant by that, she said, "You're a surveyor ain't you?" (the same old challenge that overcame my skepticism before, on the phone!)

"Well yes", I said, beginning to laugh at the situation, "but still I never learned anything in surveying about ropes, or the tying or untying of knots".

Then she handed me a paper to read; it was a briefly written description, not official in any way, but purporting to be of a small parcel of land conveyed at one time by So-and-so to So-and-so, and so forth.

"I don't see anything here about knots", I said.

"Yes you do, if you can read" (challenged again!) "It's right there, in that word 'convey'. That's what that word means—a knot, and all I want you to do is to untie the knot".

"I still don't know what you mean. The word 'convey' means to sell, or to transport".

On being told I was wrong, I asked if she had a dictionary. She brought one. Finding the dictionary to support me completely, I showed it to her. After glaring at the word and definition a moment, she declared the book to be wrong.

The hopelessness of the situation was by now evident, and a broader consideration was clearly indicated. (I should add, too, that any surveyor in such a predicament would surely begin wondering whether the afternoon was going to be a total loss!) Facing the old lady squarely, I said "Isn't there some friend of yours around here who could explain your problems to me?"

She said there was, and directed me to his place. As we drove the short distance there, Rob asked how it was going. I said,

"No use to try to tell you now, but on the way home there'll be time".

When I found the man who had charge of the old lady's affairs, he said, "Why, you poor guy, she had no business to ask you to come down here. No surveyor can help in her case". I asked him what he thought she meant by "untying the knot". That was her invariable way he said of trying to get back a piece of land she had long regretted selling. And we had a good laugh when I told him how highly she said I had been recommended to her by two local surveyors! (Confronted later, they both stoutly denied any complicity whatever—but without a convincing degree of sympathy or sobriety.)

"I hope you can collect at least a little something for your trouble in coming down here", he said. "I'll tell you what to do: just tell her that you and I have talked over her problems and that I can assure her now that everything is going to be all right, and not to worry".

When I relayed her conservator's assurances to the old lady, she seemed entirely satisfied, and asked what she owed me. When I said eight dollars, she said, "My goodness, that's a lot. I'm not sure I have that much". But in her purse she did find seven, which I assured her was fine—better than nothing at all, I thought.

On the way back to Alstead Center, Rob greatly enjoyed the humor of the whole thing. I got the impression he thought the joke was on me—not at the expense of human life in general. But in spite of it, I wondered whether the experience had left a few positive impressions.

Back at Rob's place, just before saying Goodnight as he stood by my car, he said, "You didn't ask me what I thought of the surveying business, but if you had I would have said, 'Not much'."